The Soldier's Story

D-DAY

and the Battle for Normandy

The Soldier's Story

D-DAY

and the Battle for Normandy

Compiled by
Martin Windrow

Brassey's

Copyright © 2001 Compendium Publishing Ltd

Produced by Compendium Publishing Ltd,
43 Frith Street, London W1V 5TE

This edition first published in Great Britain by
Brassey's
a division of Chrysalis Books Ltd
9 Blenheim Court
Brewery Road
London N7 9NT

A member of the Chrysalis Group plc

www.brasseys.com

ISBN 1 85753 306 2

**British Library Cataloguing
in Publication Data**
A CIP Catalogue record for this book is available
from the British Library.

Printed and bound in the United Arab Emirates

Contents

Preface

Adolf Hitler made countless mistakes during his disastrous conduct of Germany's war; but it is arguable that the most insanely self-defeating was his decision to declare war on the United States on 11 December 1941, four days after Pearl Harbor. 'Alternative history' is never anything more than an interesting intellectual game, and it is not hard to imagine other scenarios which would have brought America into the European war sooner or later; but Hitler's declaration ensured German defeat at the earliest possible moment.

Over the past twenty years there has been a tendency to become mesmerised by the sheer scale of the slaughter on the Russian Front, and consequently to write off the 1944-45 campaign in North-West Europe as secondary — even as a sideshow. This was not a mistake Hitler ever made, as his Führer Directive No. 51 of 3 November 1943 clearly shows. In the East he had a vast depth of strategic space to trade for the preservation of his armies, if he so chose. In the West his Anglo-American enemies based in Britain were little more than 300 miles — as the Fortress flies — from Germany's industrial heartland.

The consequences had the Normandy landings failed — a failure which would, by definition, have been terribly costly — are incalculable, but would certainly have set back Anglo-American ability to mount effective ground operations for at least a year. If Hitler had been able to transfer some 40 extra divisions to the East by stripping France in the aftermath of such a failure, who knows what the outcome might have been? The occupation of the USSR was by then out of the question, of course; but a damaging victory over the advancing Red Army, followed eventually by a grudging peace negotiated with his fellow dictator on something like the 1941 frontiers, is surely not inconceivable.

The Allied airborne and seaborne assault landings on the coast of Normandy launched on the night of 5/6 June 1944 were, and remain, the greatest single military operation in the history of the world, not excluding the Gulf War of 1991.

Their success was by no means assured, and the commanders who planned and led them were acutely aware of the possibility of catastrophic failure. Although this unimaginably complex operation was planned and prepared down to the last detail, and although the servicemen in the ranks seem generally to have been confident of victory, many officers from Gen Eisenhower downwards knew that once battle was joined plans would become little more than pious hopes, and that sheer luck could play as great a part as forethought and courage. On D-Day the Allies had all three on their side. In the three months which followed, as the advance from the beachhead bogged down in terribly costly fighting against the formidable reinforcements which Hitler rushed to the Invasion Front, the Allied troops needed all their reserves of courage and endurance.

This book does not pretend to offer even the briefest historical summary of the battle; such material is available in hundreds of other sources. It is specifically compiled from the words of those who were there, in an attempt to convey how ordinary individuals saw or remember their experience. Normandy was unique in a second respect. Although individuals saw only what happened in their immediate surroundings, they were aware — on the day, without having to wait for the hindsight of years — that they were taking part in an enterprise of historic importance. For some decades now younger generations have lost sight of that fact. It is ironic that it has taken the appearance of a fictional feature film — Steven Spielberg's Saving Private Ryan — to open the eyes of the young to the remarkable fund of experience which is still directly available to them through the memories of a few thousand elderly men and women in their own communities.

This collection is meant to throw light upon the soldiers' story, and very few airmen's or sailors' accounts have been included; this is, of course, no reflection on the hugely important contribution and sacrifices of those services. Some formations are heavily represented here: obviously, the assault units on D-Day, but also certain divisions — e.g. the US 2nd Armored, and British 43rd and 51st Infantry — engaged in the bocage battles of June-August. This is largely the random result of the unusual quantity and quality of memoirs and anthologies treating these units, but their experience seems to me representative of the whole.

(Simon Pugh-Jones)

Acknowledgements

Sources for text passages are listed at the back of this book; the compiler is very grateful for permission to quote copyright material. He also wishes to record his gratitude for valued assistance during the preparation of this book to — in alphabetical order — René Chartrand, Ken Ford, Lt.Col. George Forty, Simon Forty, Will Fowler, Hans Halberstadt, Jim Hooper, Bruce Robertson, Ed Storey and Steve Zaloga; for their patience, to D-Day veterans Vic 'Baseplate' Miller, Bob Murphy, Sidney Salomon and Frank Short; and for their generosity, to photographers Martin Brayley, Tim Hawkins, Tony Holmes, and Simon Pugh-Jones. Acknowledgement is also made to Tim Roop and his invaluable website: www.ww2dday.com.

Getting Ready

Within days of Japan's attack on Pearl Harbor on 7 December 1941, British Prime Minister Winston Churchill travelled to Washington to confer with President Franklin D. Roosevelt. America had been expanding its peacetime forces by conscription since September 1940, and since December that year had been providing a swelling flood of material aid to Britain under the Lend-Lease programme. She faced huge demands on her growing but then still immature resources from the Pacific war which Japan had detonated at Pearl Harbor. Nevertheless, the US government agreed on a strategy of 'Germany first'; and as early as 26 January 1942 the first US troops of the 29th Inf Div arrived in Northern Ireland.

At terrible cost, Britain and her dominions had stood alone from mid-1940 until the German invasion of the Soviet Union in mid-1941, and the subsequent Russian alliance had so far brought only theoretical benefits. Outnumbered, often defeated, bombed and almost starving, Britain remained defiant, and was fighting Germany in the air, at sea and in the North African desert; but it was only when those first GIs stepped ashore that she could clearly see the path which would lead to eventual victory.

They were the trail-blazers for a steady build-up which would see one and a half million GIs stationed in Britain by spring 1944, with newcomers finally arriving at a rate of 150,000 each month. (An incidental effect was to bring people from very different worlds into sometimes shockingly intimate contact for the first time, and to found — despite many initial misunderstandings — that 'special relationship' between the two countries which survives to this day.) From January 1943 the US 8th Army Air Force began to play its part in the strategic bombing campaign against Germany from British airfields, and the ever-increasing American air effort would be central to the Allies' domination of the skies over France in mid-1944.

The only way to defeat 'Germany first' was by the opening of a 'Second Front' through landings in continental Europe. There was considerable pressure from several quarters for a premature opening of this Second Front. In the event both the

(Tim Hawkins)

(Simon Pugh-Jones)

huge world-wide demands upon every Allied resource, and the extraordinary difficulty of mounting such an operation, delayed it until spring 1944. (The disastrous outcome of the Anglo-Canadian raid on Dieppe on 19 August 1942 underlined the dangers and difficulties of an amphibious attack on a fortified coast.)

During more than two years the whole of Britain became one vast armed camp as the expeditionary forces of Britain, the USA, Canada, and various smaller contingents from the exile armies of occupied Europe assembled and trained for the Second Front. Meanwhile the joint command — Supreme Headquarters Allied Expeditionary Forces (SHAEF), under General Dwight D. Eisenhower — proceeded with intelligence-gathering, analysis and planning on a huge scale. Finally the objective was selected: Operation 'Overlord' would set an Allied army on a 50-mile stretch of the coast of Normandy, from St Germain de Varreville in the west to Ranville in the east. That an invasion must and would take place was obvious to both sides; where and when it would be attempted was the vital secret, giving the Allies the strategic initiative. An intricate disinforma-

tion programme was launched to convince the Germans that the shorter, more obvious route from Kent to the Pas de Calais had been chosen. A parallel security operation — sometimes driven to frantic extremes — shielded the vital truth; and, remarkably, both attempts were ultimately successful. Convinced that the invasion — and even after 6 June 1944, that the 'real' invasion — would come in the Pas de Calais, Hitler would hold the vital Panzer divisions of the armoured reserve back from Normandy until they were too late to tip the balance.

Transport aircraft, troop-carrying gliders, and many types of landing ships and landing craft were produced and assembled. Special equipment and techniques were tested, on the ground, at sea and in the air; some offered promise, others failed — and many men died in the finding out. In early 1944 unprecedented numbers of tanks, half-tracks, self-propelled and towed artillery, trucks, jeeps, and every other kind of military vehicle were assembled, filling the fields of southern England alongside enormous stockpiles of weapons, fuel, munitions, equipment and consumables of every type. The plan called for 175,000 men, 1,500 tanks, 10,000 other vehicles

and 3,000 artillery pieces to be carried across the Channel and landed in the first 24 hours of the invasion. To prepare for this required, by May 1944, the efforts of a total of some $2\frac{1}{4}$ million servicemen and women in Britain.

In May 1944 the troops assigned to the invasion were marched, without warning, into southern camps which were then sealed off from all contact with the outside world. The final briefings began. The landings were originally scheduled for 5 June; when loading had already started, an unexpected deterioration in the weather led to an agonising last-minute postponement. With enormous moral courage the Supreme Commander, Gen Eisenhower, seized on the promise of a gap in the weather early on 6 June. The invasion was on.

9

'When night time came we were allowed topside and formed up and marched off the ship. There was a delegation who gave a short welcome speech and a small band playing, and after that was over we marched through the streets of Liverpool to the railroad station. This was my first view of any war damage or anything and I was fascinated, looking ... at the ruins of buildings and the rubble in the streets, block after block. This was as a result of the Blitz, of course.'
Pfc Vernon W. Tart,
174th Ordnance Battalion,
US 6th Engineer Special Bde (1)

'I finally adopted the Princes, or should I say they adopted me? I spent practically all of my off-time at their home and usually had my Sunday dinner with them. At first I felt quite embarassed when I ate their food, knowing they were strictly rationed, but when I found I could repay them with surplus sugar, butter, flour and fruit from our own company kitchen, I didn't feel so bad about it. Under the Army system of food logistics, there could be no leftovers, and, if there were, the officers of the company didn't object to the boys taking them to friends in town ... I wrote to my wife, Betty, and explained the situation and she began sending packages containing food and other odds and ends not available in Britain.'
Pte George McIntyre,
4th Engineer Bn,
US 4th Infantry Division (2)

'Naturally, the first place many of us headed for were the English pubs. We found the barkeeps friendly and honest, an important factor when you consider we didn't know the true value of English pennies, shillings and pounds ... Pubs are nothing less than the working men's club, where people gather to discuss weather, politics or crops over a glass of beer.'
Pte George McIntyre,
4th Engineer Bn,
US 4th Inf Div (3)

The sight of civilian housing ravaged by unrestricted aerial bombing was new and shocking to the GIs arriving in England's port cities. (Imperial War Museum HU635)

(Tim Hawkins)

'Small booklets were published and distributed to each American soldier, telling him how to 'get along' with the British ... Pubs are a tremendous factor in Anglo-American relations. In my own experience and among my own close personal friends, I know of countless cases of Englishmen establishing extremely cordial relations with our boys ... The so-called British reserve breaks down completely inside of a pub. A lot of friendships and a lot of real understanding is developed over a glass of beer.

'Of course, by the same token, pubs are wonderful places for a fight ... That is to be expected. Because after a man gets a few drinks under his belt, he forgets all the little lessons in Anglo-American relations he learned in the booklet.'

**Maj Thor M. Smith,
SHAEF staff (4)**

'Our training was rough, we never had nothing easy. We would get up and run four miles in twenty minutes and this was before breakfast. We would have to run two or three mile obstacle courses with some of the damnedest obstacles ... No one realized how horrible our training was. We would take two or three thirty-mile hikes a week ... The fog was so low and thick that if you stood ... straight up you could probably see no more than four or five feet ... I was born in Charlottesville, Virginia, and I was never in the northern part of the country ... where the cold is. The higher you went on the moors the deeper the swamp got. It would be covered with blocks of ice at times and it was miserably cold.'

**Pte Felix Branham,
116th Inf Regt,
US 29th Inf Div (5)**

(Tim Hawkins)

11

'We came to know, but never to love Dartmoor, as we tramped across it, shivered in its cold winds and slept on its liquid surface. One attack called for overhead machine gunfire using live ammunition. We put wooden stops under the gun barrels to be sure they would not accidentally be depressed, but just as the firing started an umpire came along and kicked away the stops, saying they ruined the realism. This particular bow to realism has played on my mind ever since, for somehow a muzzle dropped and a burst of fire hit in among some riflemen, killing one. It was the battalion's first such death in training, but not the last; casualties rose as live ammunition and high explosives played a large part in training to kill...'

Lt Charles Cawthon, 2nd Bn, 116th Inf Regt, US 29th Inf Div (6)

'Many will say that our training, the majority of which took place in Kent with its many small exercises and 36-mile route marches, was physically harder than the real thing.'

Sgt C. G. Deal, 4th Bn, Dorsetshire Regt, British 43rd Inf Div (7)

'What I always remembered about those marches was just a short time into them your boots would get to feeling like they weighed a ton. The canteen beating on one hip would have you really tee'd off. A commando knife on the other hip, bouncing up and down ... the hand grenade bouncing on your belly didn't help any. The rifle sling digging into your shoulder and the helmet on your head bouncing up and down, beating your brains out ... The only thing I can say is that it's amazing what a guy will go through for his country.'

Pte William C. Smith, 2nd Bn, 115th Inf Regt, US 29th Inf Div (8)

'A British gliders training camp nearby appeared wasteful of life to the point of disregard; few days passed, it seemed, that a caisson bearing a flag-draped coffin, escorted by troopers in red berets, did not rumble by ...'

Lt Charles Cawthon, 2nd Bn, 116th Inf Regt, US 29th Inf Div (9)

'We had quite a few people killed while we were training in gliders; I was nearly killed myself. Coming back from a flight over the sea ... I think we got caught in the slipstream of aircraft ahead of us and the glider started to whirl about and suddenly the tow-rope broke while we were still about three or four miles out to sea ... so we had to prepare for ditching ... It took about four or five minutes to get down ...

'We also had on board an RAF wing commander ... he was bracing himself against the same bulkhead as me and looked absolutely terrified. He'd probably

ditched in the sea before and knew what it was like ... Actually, it's amazing how hard water is, it's like running into a brick wall at eighty miles an hour ... The pilot and myself and all the people in the front of the glider just shot out the front of the thing, straight through the fuselage. Next thing I can remember is actually waking up under water ... I couldn't move my legs much because I had smashed my back and neck a bit. The glider floated for a while and we all got back on it until we were picked up by a Walrus flying boat.'

Capt John Tillett, 2nd Bn, Ox. & Bucks. Light Infantry, British 6th Abn Div (10)

All over Britain during 1943–44 tens of thousands of machines and hundreds of thousands of men and women practised endlessly for every foreseeable aspect of the forthcoming Second Front. In May 1944 they filtered south, filling the fields and roads of southern England as they moved into their marshalling areas.
(US National Archives)

(Tim Hawkins)

'Our role was to learn the use of [DD Sherman] swimming tanks ... The tactical training was extended, repetitive and dull, but a few weeks in Normandy soon made me realise that our then CO taught us most thoroughly ... The technical training ... involved launching the vehicles from landing craft ramps - at which we became remarkably proficient in all seas, for which the vehicles had not been designed ...

'At the same time we were given training in the Davis Submarine Escape Apparatus ... We sat in an old tank turret at the bottom of a deep pit and thousands of gallons of water poured on to us, giving us just a few seconds to don the apparatus...

'There was a lot of experimenting with tank stability vis-à-vis the necessity of loading as much ammunition as possible along with a variety of supplies never conceived by us before ... We put in so many extra fittings — racks around the turrets for shells and so on — that we had to have a full-scale exercise to see if the wretched things would still float ... Admiral Ramsay (who commanded the whole show) had a brainwave that each tank should have an inflatable rubber dinghy — and to this I owe my D Day life, as I am a non-swimmer.'

Tpr M. E. Mawson,
13th/18th Royal Hussars,
British 27th Armd Bde (11)

'Most of the early exercises were pretty catastrophic. All sorts of things went wrong, but we were learning ... Vehicles broke down. Coming off a landing craft in a tank, when the sea is rough, isn't particularly easy, and sometimes we'd get a vehicle broken down on the ramp of the LCT and it had to be towed off... We certainly needed training ... You can't talk to any of your subordinate tanks without wireless and we'd never used that, and we were very verbose ... but as we got more confident in it we got far quicker — people recognize your voice and you cut everything down, so that in the end conversations were just click click click and you knew exactly what the men meant.'

Maj R. Younger, British
Royal Engineers, commanding a

Two weeks before the invasion, a staff sergeant of the 175th Inf Regt, US 29th Inf Div hones his knife in a tented camp near Falmouth in Cornwall. Adding the huge numbers of support and service personnel to the combat divisions, some two million men and women were sealed off from the outside world — without prior warning — by barbed wire and vigilant MPs. (US National Archives)

'In the meantime we were having assault training schools. We swam through tanks of water with full equipment on. We threw various hand grenades. We were shown various ... enemy weapons and how we could use them if we landed and misplaced our weapons. They would show us how to attack pillboxes, what to do if we became separated ...

'I joined a demolition team. I carried a 50-pound pole charge and a 50-pound satchel charge made of burlap and TNT. I figured "OK, if I make the Second Front and I get hit with all the explosives I would be carrying, then it would all be over real quick." If it had to be, that's the way I wanted it to be.'

Pte Felix Branham, 116th Inf Regt, US 29th Inf Div (13)

'Our training was hard but purposeful, we were being whipped into a real fighting unit. Our officers and NCOs did their job well, we were really good and we knew it. I had taken over a Bren gun ... I reckoned I was the best there was, my reflexes were quick, my work rate was high and I was very fleet of foot. There was a certain rapport between all ranks which is difficult to describe. No one dared let our Platoon Commander down, or they were never allowed to forget it, we were behind [him] to a man.'

**Pte Albert Kings,
1st Bn, Worcestershire Regt,
British 43rd Inf Div (14)**

'Amphibious training began in earnest when the regiment moved to tented camps in Hampshire. The training area was selected because it resembled the terrain and beaches of Normandy. Slapton Sands near Dartmouth was a sloping expanse of sand and shingle guarded by an armpit-deep salt marsh which had to be crossed before assaulting simulated fortified bunkers. The company hiked all day dripping wet ... and slept that night in the same damp clothes. It was one of the most miserable experiences I can remember as a soldier ...

'Dry runs preceded the actual drills. Mock-up landing craft and cargo nets set the stage ... Nets were hung from high makeshift walls and the troops practised climbing them with full field equipment ...

'Crawling under barbed wire with live machine-gun ... fire just inches overhead and live explosions, strategically placed, detonating all around, lent realism to these exercises.'

**Sgt John R. Slaughter, 1st Bn,
116th Inf Regt, US 29th Inf Div
(15)**

'[We] went out in the Channel one week in a convoy ... that got torpedoed by German E-Boats. We lost five of the nine

end was knocked off the one that I was on. I was down in the hold with the vehicles, gasoline and ammunition just packed in there. I heard one torpedo come sliding down the side of the hull, but it didn't explode. Then the next one caught the stern end and tore off about thirty feet ... It was like there was a big door back there, but we didn't sink. I managed to get up on top. The tracer bullets were thick as hair on a dog's back ...

'We just sat there the rest of the night, trying to keep all the GIs under control ... pleading and begging to get them to stay in place ... Next morning a British tug boat came out and pushed us into Plymouth ... Nothing was ever said about it ... They wouldn't let anybody see us or talk to us or anything for a week or two, then they sent us back to our company.'

**Sgt Ewell B. Lunsford, 4th Medical
Bn, US 4th Inf Div (16)**

'Them Germans slipped in there and sunk the hell out of them couple of LSTs and we lost them 740 men. And after that tragedy there that night, we were impounded and they swore they'd cut our damn heads off if we divulged it ... Later they said it would be a breakdown of morale to the other soldiers ...'

**Pte Sam Jacks, US 83rd
Field Arty Bn (17)**

Vehicles of the US 29th Inf Div unload from a Landing Ship Tank (LST) onto a Rhino ferry for a pre-invasion exercise at Slapton Sands, Devonshire, in late March 1944. During the exercise of 27/28 April, Operation 'Tiger', German torpedo boats got among the transports, sank two LSTs and damaged others. A succession of errors led to some 750 men being killed and 300 wounded. (US National Archives)

(Martin Brayley)

(Tim Hawkins)

shoved under barbed wire to blow a pathway. The next men were designated as wire cutters ... Then came machine gunners to cover us, next 60mm mortar gunners and ammo carriers. Lastly, a flamethrower team and a dynamite team to get close to the pillbox and blow it up.

'One of the boys set off a charge that had a short fuse. It blew up in his face. I was glad I didn't see him, thank God. They said he still had his helmet strap down below his chin and after that we never wore our helmet straps buckled except for parades and guard duty [in order to avoid decapitation].'

Pfc John Barnes, 1st Bn, 116th Inf Regt, US 29th Inf Div (18)

'One particular "scheme" carried out in early 1944 was the worst I ever recall. The weather was bitterly cold, it rained incessantly; we fought our way from Stone Street mostly across country through muddy fields and almost impassable tracks. Many men suffered from exhaustion. The company issued with bicycles found them clogging up completely with mud. When taken to Normandy the experience was the same and all [the bicycles] were abandoned a few miles from the coast. I recall a complete platoon blown up on Dymchurch beach on a demonstration of the Hawkins 77 anti-tank mines used as anti-personnel mines.'

Cpl Leo Davis, 4th Bn, Somerset Light Infantry, British 43rd Inf Div (19)

'Out on the moors we would practice landings from an imaginary boat. Men would line up in three columns, ten men each. The first three out of the boat were riflemen. They would fan out when the ramp went down and take up protective fire positions. Next came two men who carried bangalore torpedoes, long lengths of pipe containing dynamite ...

(Tim Hawkins)

'A little group of us ... passed what seemed to be a social club in a kind of hall and there were dustbins on one side and some American soldiers, coloured men, were emptying their mess tins and they were throwing chicken away. Well, most of us hadn't seen any chicken for years and we stopped and stared ... a chap came out — it turned out later he was the QM — and asked us if we had eaten ... He fed us with all the chicken that they were going to ditch. It was all good stuff, too. Afterwards they gave us ice cream and apologized that all they had left in the barrel was vanilla. They apologized! I don't suppose any of us had seen ice cream since before the war.'

**L/Cpl John Bailey,
Ox. & Bucks. Light Infantry,
British 6th Abn Div (20)**

'[The guns] were having their final waterproofing and welding done. The waterproofing was done with the aid of a sealing compound, new to most of us, called Bostik. The kits had to be cut to shape, and with scissors thoughtfully provided. The most bizarre feature of the waterproofing was a kind of square (or rather oblong in section) chimney or funnel that stuck up like a wren's tail out of the rear of the SP (and likewise tanks) just above the engines so that water should not be able to flood them. Drivers, who were also sealed in, had been trained to drive with the water up to their ears — or thereabouts. But the funnels were a great deal taller than that, possibly in case waves splashed over the top. After landing the funnels, or shutes as they were also known, were to be blown off with an explosive charge; otherwise the engines would have overheated.'

**2nd Lt Sidney Rosenbaum, British
Royal Artillery, commanding
a troop of self-propelled guns (21)**

'Every field and vacant lot was piled high with matériel for an impending great battle. Tanks and other tracked vehicles; trucks, jeeps and weapons carriers; spotter Piper Cub airplanes; artillery pieces of all sizes; gasoline, water, food, jerry cans, boxes, drums, you name it and it was there, in abundance.'

**Sgt John R. Slaughter,
1st Bn, 116th Inf Regt,
US 29th Inf Div (22)**

'Once we had been given our first briefing and knew the LZ and the glider targets, a tight security clamp was imposed. No one was allowed off the camp, no letters were collected though we received incoming mail, and no telephone calls were permitted. Even an ENSA concert party arriving by coach was turned away ... During these days we studied photographs, large-scale maps and then we got a sand table of the coastline with the river Orne running up to Caen. We were even shown a film of the run-in from the coastline to the LZ. I think much of the success of the final operation was due to these visual aids we were given in the last few days.'

**Flt Lt P. M. Bristow,
No 575 Squadron RAF (23)**

'At the end of May 1944, I was in command of a company of the 13th Parachute Battalion (Lancashire). We were one day whisked away to a place unknown but quickly termed by all ranks as the Concentration Camp. This concentration did not concern, to my mind, the numbers of troops in one spot so much as the amount of briefing, checking and counter-checking down to the last detail, almost down to each man's individual role in the forthcoming invasion. We learned here that the objective of the 6th Airborne was Normandy — in a part so very much resembling the country round Oxon-Gloucester-Wiltshire borders where so much of our training over the past months had been carried out.'

**Capt A. R. Clark, 13th Parachute
Bn, British 6th Abn Div (24)**

(Martin Brayley)

'As a lecturer and trained member of a camouflage unit of 21st Army Group HQ, I was attached to No 9 Beach Group ... Quite suddenly I was summoned to a meeting ... and met other members of a team with whom I was to work for the next few days under closest security; an armed guard in fact. We were to make a model of No 9 Beach Group landing area in Normandy. The 12 feet by 12 feet model had to be accurate ... various units were to be briefed from it ... A mosaic of photographs from all angles came in plentiful supply. Up-to-date information on enemy defences was readily available ... Our particular concern was the stretch of beach at Ver-sur-Mer, between Courseulles and Arromanches.

'I remember well the landmarks ... the pale-toned ribbon of road, leading at right angles from the coastline ... the white silhouette of the lighthouse, the pink walls of a chateau near the beach and several concrete ... gun emplacements. Eventually ... the model was finished and the personnel from all units of the Beach Group were briefed for their hazardous adventure of storming the beaches.'
V.J.Galliano, 21st Army Group HQ (26)

'One day a fence was put up around the camp. The NCOs were sent for and told that anyone caught outside would be court-martialled. Nobody got out. We had the best briefing I have ever known in the forces; even the private soldiers were present. There were scale models, photographs of guns, minefields and so on.'
Sgt George Self, 8th Bn, Durham Light Infantry, British 50th Inf Div (27)

A US Army chaplain holds a field service in a hospital area, accompanied by a nurse seated at a portable organ. (US National Archives)

'My personal emotions and feelings on knowing I would be amongst the first British troops to land in France started a few years before the actual Day. During the chaotic exercises and seeing the Heath Robinson equipment and the lives lost in practice made me wonder if we would ever leave Britain. However, when I was put in the concentration camp near the south coast, shown photographs and briefed individually on my particular task, and listened to Monty giving his talk and explanation of the operation, I felt confident and optimistic as to how easy it would be.'
Dvr A. O. Palser, 246 Field Co, British Royal Engineers (25)

Gen Omar Bradley (right), commanding US 1st Army, addresses officers of the 29th Inf Div near Tavistock, Devonshire, in late March 1944. (US National Archives)

'The air photographs were very clear, and it would not have taken much enterprise to pick out the place on the map of France. However, we were asked not to do so. The Free French troops in the unit nearly all recognized the area at once. Some of them even lived in the area, and had been in the town less than a year before. One used to work the lock gates at the mouth of the canal before the war.

'The endless conferences were rather tedious, and to my mind a bit overdone. Anyone who had been in action before could feel that such detailed planning was rather a waste of time. Personally, I refused to be tied down to much detail in my plans, knowing full well that things would look very different when the time came. When they tried to pin me down to which house I was to make my RAP (Regimental Aid Post), I drew the line completely.'

Capt J. H. Patterson, medical officer, 4 Cdo, British 1st Special Service Bde (28)

'The inspection over, [Gen Montgomery] took up his familiar position on top of some army vehicle and called us to gather round in an informal manner. He then told us in his characteristic way, that we were going to land in France, knock Jerry for six, and finish the war off. There was absolutely no doubt about it — it was all planned and organized. We would just go in, do the job, and that was that. There was something so tremendously impressive, almost hypnotic, in his performance, that it did inspire us with a confidence which in retrospect was not at all justified. It was the sheer matter-of-fact certainty of his message that was so much more effective than a high-flown Harfleur-type effort.'

Pte Tom Tateson, 7th Bn, Green Howards, British 50th Inf Div (29)

'Montgomery visited us and told us that 50 Div would be one of the leading divisions in the invasion. Morale dropped for a few moments. After he had gone, there was a lot of discussion about divisions lying about in the country that had never been on active service, and how it was not right that we should do the invasion. People were bitter. We had done plenty of fighting; let someone else have a go. There were no problems with discipline, but a lot of moaning. About 50 per cent didn't like him, although they accepted him as a leader.'

Sgt George Self, 8th Bn, Durham Light Infantry, British 50th Inf Div (30)

(Martin Brayley)

Gen Bernard Montgomery (left), commander of the British/Canadian 21st Army Group and overall commander of Allied ground forces for the assault phase of the invasion, visiting Gen Maczek's 1st Polish Armd Div, which would reinforce his army in Normandy at the end of July, and would play a central role in trapping German forces in the so-called 'Falaise Pocket'. (IWM MH1400)

(Martin Brayley)

The Allies' continuing fear that the Germans might resort to chemical warfare led them not only to insist on men carrying gas masks, but also to outfit them with variously impregnated clothing which was supposed to have a protective effect against chemical agents. The troops' opinion of such kit was unanimous:

'Our uniforms were regular fatigues that had been impregnated chemically against gas. They felt very stiff and uncomfortable and odoriferous. The old canvas lace-up leggings still worn at the time received the same treatment. I reckon the Krauts would have smelt us coming ...'
Pte John Lynch, US 30th Inf Div (31)

'They were the lousiest, the coldest, the clammiest, the stiffest, the stinkiest articles of clothing that were ever dreamed up ...'
Pte Edward Jeziorski, 507th Parachute Inf Regt, US 82nd Abn Div (32)

'The whole outfit now has a very bad case of the invasion shakes. Very little talk about anything but assault landings, what it will be like, what the casualties will be, etc. any way you look at it, it's not going to be any piece of cake. After the alert this morning, I caught myself several times looking around and wondering for the hundredth time how the hell I got here ...'
S/Sgt J. Giles, US 291st Combat Engineer Bn (33)

'[The operation plan for the regiment] was thicker than the biggest telephone book you've ever seen. After the briefing was completed Col Good stood up, he picked it up and tried to tear it in half, but it was so thick that this strong man couldn't do it. So he simply threw it over his shoulder and said, "Forget this goddamned thing. You get your ass on the beach. I'll be there waiting for you and I'll tell you what to do. There ain't anything in this plan that is going to go right."
Capt Robert Miller, 175th Inf Regt, US 29th Inf Div (34)

Getting There By Air
US Airborne

The first Allied combat troops to arrive on the soil of occupied France in the early hours of 6 June were the men of the three airborne divisions — some 13,400 paratroopers and 'glider-riders' of the US 82nd and 101st, and 6,255 British and Canadians of the British 6th Airborne. Their task (which some senior commanders considered to be little more than a suicide mission) was to seize strategic objectives inland from the invasion beaches — particularly river crossings — to ensure that enemy counter-attacks could not pin the amphibious troops at the edge of the sea, and that the beachhead could be expanded rapidly. They would have to hold these objectives, with the slim resources available to any airborne force, until the amphibious troops fought their way ashore and inland to join them.

The US 82nd Abn Div would be dropped on both banks of the Merderet river south and west of Ste Mère-Eglise, north of Carentan on a vital road axis which the Germans would have to use for reinforcement of the Cotentin Peninsula. The 101st would be dropped slightly south and east, to seize the exit routes from the westernmost landing beach, codenamed 'Utah', and the crossings of the Douve river. Their missions were complicated by the fact that the Germans had deliberately flooded large areas of the shallow valleys of the Merderet and Douve, limiting the usable routes to causeways through marshland under standing water of uncertain depth.

Despite the most meticulous preparation, any massed parachute landing is inevitably vulnerable to confusion and missed schedules, and the difficulties of a night drop multiply these problems many times. The pilots of the 822 C-47 transport aircraft carrying the 82nd and 101st across the Channel — low, slow, in close formation, and in the dark — were not combat-experienced. They overreacted to the German anti-aircraft fire they encountered over the coast, and were disoriented by an unexpected cloud bank. Their evasive manoeuvres led to a high proportion of the US airborne units being dropped in the wrong places and widely scattered. Significant numbers dropped into the floods, and drowned; a few fell right into German gunsights around Ste Mère-Eglise, and were shot as they dangled helplessly.

Large and small groups, often of officers and men from mixed-up units and usually lacking their heavy weapons, found each other in the dark by luck or judgement. They tried to work out where they were, and whether they could salvage some part of their operation plans. Under these nightmare circumstances they performed outstandingly in a series of confused night encounter battles, in which the enemy were handicapped by the sheer incoherence of the reported landings. Some troopers were left to their own devices for days; but enough managed to assemble into *ad hoc* units to achieve their vital objectives: the exits from Utah Beach, and the vital bridges, were secured.

(Left) On the evening of 5 June at Greenham Common airfield, Gen Dwight D. Eisenhower — Supreme Commander Allied Expeditionary Forces, and the man bearing the greatest burden of responsibility for the largest military operation in history — mingles with men of the US 101st Airborne Division shortly before they emplane for Normandy. (US National Archives)

'After blackening our faces, sharpening our knives and checking our equipment for the 100th time, we got into formation and walked to the airfield. This was about 10pm. On the way to the airfield we were swinging along, some of us singing, and a little old Cockney lady ran up and said "Give 'em hell, Yanks." A lump came into my throat, both of fear and pride.'

**Lt Parker A. Alford, 3rd Bn,
501st Parachute Inf Regt,
US 101st Abn Div (1)**

'We had gotten to our aerodrome around three or four o'clock on the afternoon of June 5. Briefing was over; everybody having been briefed and briefed again. Now, everyone was on hand. All officers were there with the men of their particular section, casually going over plans and alternate plans, checking maps, technical equipment, etc. ... There was no visible sign of nervousness, tenseness, brooding, doubt, and certainly not fear. Time and again we had gone through this very same procedure in our training to equip ourselves for the moment so near at hand ...'

**Sgt Thomas B. Buff, Headquarters,
US 101st Abn Div (2)**

'There is no greater bore than waiting around to go into combat. You know damned well there is nothing you can do to change anything. Everyone sweats it out in his own way. We all put on a happy face for appearance's sake. I observed one young replacement who was really down. I got the company "barber kit" out and told him he needed a haircut, that I wanted him to look good when we entered Paris. I was able to talk him out of his funk ... I assured him that every man in that hangar was as scared as he was, including myself. I feel I relieved him of some of his anxiety. I hope so anyway; he was one of the first killed.'

**Sgt William T. Dunfee,
3rd Bn, 505th PIR,
US 82nd Abn Div (3)**

(Tim Hawkins)

(Tim Hawkins)

21

'[I was wearing] one suit of olive drab, worn underneath my jump suit ... helmet, boots, gloves, main parachute, reserve parachute, Mae West [inflatable life jacket], rifle, .45 automatic pistol, trench knife, jump knife, hunting knife, machete, one cartridge belt, two bandoliers, two cans of machine-gun ammo totalling 676 rounds of .30 ammo, 66 rounds of .45 ammo, one Hawkins mine capable of blowing off the tracks of a tank, four blocks of TNT, one entrenching tool with two blasting caps taped on the outside of the steel part, three first aid kits, two morphine needles, one gas mask, a canteen of water, three days' supply of K-rations, two days' supply of D-rations, six fragmentation grenades, one Gammon grenade [anti-tank grenade of bagged plastic explosive], one orange smoke and one red smoke grenade, one orange [marker] panel, one blanket, one raincoat, one change of socks and underwear, two cartons of cigarettes and a few other odds and ends...'

Pte Donald Burgett, 506th PIR, US 101st Abn Div (4)

Waco troop-carrying glider (foreground) and a formation of C-47 transport aircraft. The C-47 carried between 18 and 24 paratroopers depending upon what heavy equipment was also loaded. The Douglas C-47, an unglamorous workhorse of an aircraft, nevertheless made as great a contribution to Allied victory as the Flying Fortress. (US National Archives)

'First thing we did, flying over, was pitch our gas masks out the door ... We figured the Germans wouldn't use gas and we didn't want to jump with the darn thing. It wraps around you and it's an uncomfortable thing to carry. The English Channel must be full of gas masks, thousands of them.

'As the time was getting closer I was getting nervous, getting butterflies in my stomach. I was hoping I wouldn't run into the same problem we had when we were making our drop into Sicily and our own navy shot us down by mistake ... During our briefing we were told that the entire coast of France was mined ... fields were flooded, poles were stuck in the ground to keep our gliders from coming in. So we didn't know what to expect and of course we expected the worst ...

'Then one man gets air sick and pulls his steel helmet off to heave into it. And then everybody else down the line follows suit. Everybody is heaving, dry heaves, waiting, waiting to get out of that aeroplane. We are all sick and the plane stinks and we are ready to get out any time ...

'When the time came to go, out the door we went. We didn't hesitate for one moment. We were happy to get out of that thing ... Yes, I was afraid. I was nineteen years old and I was afraid.'

Pte George Alex, US 82nd Abn Div (5)

Troopers of the **US 82nd Abn Div** 'chute up'. Their two parachute packs and their massive loads of weapons, munitions, rations, and every other necessity to enable them to fight alone and unsupported, so confined and weighed down the paratroopers that they could hardly walk, and needed help to board the aircraft. (US Army)

'As we approached our area to jump, some of the paratroopers ... were dozing when a line of tracer bullets cut through the length of the fuselage of the C-47 causing men sitting on either side to pull their feet in closer. No one was hit, but it got their attention fast so that everyone was fully alert for the next surprise — a direct hit on the left engine. Immediately, Lt John Evans yelled, "Stand up and hook up!" ... No sooner were we in place when a third hit took off part of the right wing. The plane tilted down and to the right. Lt Evans yelled, "GO!" and led the way. That was the last time anyone ever saw or heard from Evans. I recall I was the twenty-fourth man and last to leave the plane, and remember how the plane was going down. I moved as fast as I could to get out and, after baling out, saw the plane go up in a ball of flame.'

Jack Schlegel, 3rd Bn, 508th PIR, US 82nd Abn Div (6)

'The first twelve men got out pretty close together. I was running down the aisle. Suddenly the plane was hit in the left wing by flak. The wing went straight up. My left shoulder crashed into a window. With ammo, a 1903 Springfield rifle, twelve grenade-launcher rounds, two cans of blood plasma, two cans of distilled water, gas mask, helmet, K-rations, I must have weighed 225-250 pounds ... I was surprised the window didn't break. The pilot was fighting to right the plane. When he succeeded, I was appalled at the view which greeted me — I was the only one standing. Four men lay in a tangled heap on the floor. I realized it was almost impossible for them to stand up with their equipment loads. Also that an absolute sequence had to be maintained or we'd have a glob of human hamburger dangling outside the door at 150 miles an hour. One man dived out of the door head first. I stepped over the top of two men. The closest man to the door crawled out head first. I grabbed the ... man I thought next and gave him a heave out nose first. The next man made it crawling on his own power. I reached up and pulled the salvo switch which released the machine gun and mortars attached to the bomb racks of the plane, then I dived out.'

Sgt Louis E. Traux, 1st Bn, 506th PIR, US 101st Abn Div (7)

'With the plane on fire, in a dive, the pilot and co-pilot slumped forward and the crew chief unable to determine our position, I gave the order to go. I estimated our altitude between 350 and 400 feet. When my 'chute opened ... I had two oscillations in the air and then hit the ground hard somewhere in France ... I readied my weapon ... and removed my 'chute ready to engage the enemy — which turned out to be a big white horse ... I collected my gear and proceeded to the edge of the field and started down the hedgerow to collect the jump stick. From the amount of firing it was obvious that a sizeable German force was between me and the men who had jumped with me ... I saw an enemy patrol on the other side so I ... let them pass and then [got] into position for a fire fight. I then back-tracked, hoping to find someone from my group. . . but to no avail. I then surmised that the men in my stick had landed among enemy troops and I had landed on the fringe of an enemy bivouac.'

Howard Hugget, 326th Abn Engineer Bn, US 101st Abn Div (8)

'I don't know how high our plane was, but I'm sure it was very low because I remember swinging about twice and then landing in the middle of a road ... I took about two steps and went head first through a wooden fence, knocking out two teeth and cutting my lip. I rolled over, tried to get my carbine out, couldn't, sat up, and ... finally got out of my harness ... [I] pulled my folding stock carbine out and could hear some soldiers coming down the road ... [It] felt like someone was holding me by the belt ... and I found the shroud lines ... tangled up in the fence. I could hear the boots getting closer and closer. I finally got the shroud lines unhooked, climbed to the top of the hedgerow, fell over the other side, and in about a minute 35 to 40 Germans came marching past. I could have reached out and touched them. Being alone behind enemy lines is a unique, indescribable feeling. You just feel so helpless, so alone that there is nothing in your life you can relate it to.'

George Rosie, 506th PIR, US 101st Abn Div (9)

'The sky seemed alive with tracer, red and green and pink, floating up and snapping past. In the distance ... I could see a sizeable fire, a house in Ste Mère-Eglise, though I didn't know it at the time ... I hid in an apple orchard ... cleared my harness, put my rifle together, but I could not find any sign of life except some firing from down the road. Our stick leader had been immediately captured and was later killed by our own aircraft in a strafing attack. Another aircraft, flaming like a comet, crashed in a field nearby and I thought of the troopers on board. I later saw a C-47 down in the marshes of the Merderet river. The area into which we jumped was occupied by the tightly disciplined 91st German Division, and they occupied most of the farms. We were also surprised at the immense size of the hedgerows. No one had told us about the flooded marshes. I had no idea where the hell I was and I could not find my stick, but I was alive.'

D. Zane Schlemmer, 2nd Bn, 508th PIR, US 82nd Abn Div (10)

US paratroopers take cover in a roadside ditch in Normandy; in the background, a shot-up German truck. The scattered air drops meant that small groups of US Airborne troopers had to fight a whole series of isolated battles with whatever means they had to hand before linking up with the rest of their units. Some men from the 82nd Abn Div, dropped astride the flooded Merderet river, had to hold out without support for four days. (US National Archives)

(Tim Hawkins)

'By the time Jim joined me I had the bundle unrolled and the bazooka and ammo out. We loaded up and headed for Ste Mère-Eglise. It was easy to locate — that's where most of the firing was coming from ... we heard what sounded like a box-car flying through the air and hit the deck. I think it was a 16-inch naval shell that hit in a field nearby. It rained chunks of earth and rock for what seemed like several minutes.

'Jim and I joined a group on the outskirts of Ste Mère-Eglise. Our battalion commander, Lt Col 'Cannonball' Krause, ordered all bazookas forward ... Establishing a perimeter defensive position, we dug in to await the counter-attack that came all too swiftly. The enemy really socked it to us with SSs and "screaming meemies". The SSs were using either timed or proximity fuses, because we were receiving air-bursts. The Nebelwerfers were so erratic you couldn't tell where their rockets would land ...

'We suffered a number of casualties during this bombardment. The most gruesome was when a rocket landed among three men in a mortar squad. They were all killed and the explosion must have detonated a "Gammon grenade" in one of the men's pockets, for the secondary explosion literally blew him to bits. His head, chest and right arm were all that remained.'

Sgt William T. Dunfee, 3rd Bn, 505th PIR, US 82nd Abn Div (12)

'In the moonlight it looked like a nice smooth meadow to land in, but instead it was a splash ... The wind was blowing the 'chute and I took in a lot of water before I got myself cut loose ... Several of us got to a railway causeway which cut through the swamp ... part of the Merderet river flood plain. We followed the railroad ... to a road. At dawn, along came a German motorcyclist. Several of us fired, and we figured it would have taken three strong men to carry him to a grave with all that lead in him. He was being followed by a staff car which managed to ... get away ... Later we met up with our Divisional Commander, Major-General Matthew B. Ridgeway, and Brigadier-General Gavin, who we had jumped with, and about a hundred others. The enemy got us pretty well located — they were good — and gave us a bit of hell with mortar and small-arms fire, including snipers. We had a few prisoners ... about twenty — including a few officers of field grade. All in all, it wasn't a bad day for our plane-load. We all made it and I considered that a miracle of some sort.'

Leslie Kick, Headquarters, US 82nd Abn Div (11)

(Tim Hawkins)

(Tim Hawkins)

'We saw not only our own platoon go, but so many others drown in the river. They had so much equipment on them and no quick release 'chutes in those days: if you landed in a flooded river you got drowned ... Others got caught in the trees and then shot whilst they were hanging there ... they were just left there hanging ... It was devastating.'

Lt Henry Lefebvfre, 1st Bn, 508th PIR, US 82nd Abn Div (14)

'[Our medic Anderson] was hanging in a tree by his feet, his arms down, throat cut, genitals stuffed in his mouth. His medic's red cross armband was stained with the blood that had flowed from his hair.'

Lt Carl Cartledge, 501st PIR, US 101st Abn Div (15)

'I had landed in front of a German bunker, about thirty yards away, but someone who had hit the ground before me had dropped a Gammon grenade in it and put it out of order ... I lay against the bank for a short while, then saw two Germans approaching on the other side of the hedgerow. We had orders not to load our weapons until we were organized, so my carbine was not loaded. As the Germans approached I fully intended to let them go by, but just in case I unscrewed the [safety] cap of my Gammon grenade.

'When they got just opposite me they noticed me and ducked ... one of them started slowly rising. I saw the top of his head and when I saw his shoulders I threw the Gammon grenade. At the same time he fired and a bullet passed through the crotch of my outsize pair of pants. The muzzle blast knocked me out and when I came to my face was in the bank, in the dirt, my mouth was open and blood and spit were trickling out. I could hear but I couldn't move. I thought I was dead and that this was the way people died. I heard moaning on the other side of the hedgerow, so I knew my grenade had had some effect ...

'I was lying on my back in the dry brush, my trench knife under me and my carbine off to my left when I heard two Germans approaching. You could tell Germans by the amount of leather they wore; you could hear it creak as they walked. They stood over me and looked down at me. There wasn't anything I could do, just play dead. I waited. I had to go to the bathroom very badly and I went. It's quite possible the Germans mistook what they saw for blood. After a while I opened my eyes and saw they had gone, so I crawled deeper down to the bottom of the gully and...went to sleep.'

Pte Harold Canyon, 2nd Bn, 508th PIR, US 82nd Abn Div (13)

'Basically we hit pretty close to where we were supposed to be, but we were very scattered. I was completely alone. There was a farmhouse back up about 150 yards from where I dropped, so I snuck up to it and inside I could hear Germans talking. I was going to sneak away ... when one of them came out to check what was going on. He came round the corner. I was standing flat against the wall and I killed my first German right there. I hit him on the side of the head with my rifle butt, then gave him the bayonet treatment. Then I took off, ran like hell.'

Sgt Dan Furlong, 508th PIR,
US 82nd Abn Div (16)

(Left) A medic gives a wounded paratrooper a smoke; his rifle is thrust into the ground to support a plasma bottle as they prepare to transfuse him. Casualty and fatality rates among airborne troops were always higher than among conventional infantry. Not only were their isolated missions and light armament inherently more dangerous; they were also often unable to evacuate their wounded in time for them to receive life-saving treatment.
(US National Archives)

'Just at that moment the hatch of the tank opened and raised back and the tank commander climbed up to where his waist was out of the tank and he was looking round. [Sgt Ray] Hummle dropped the Gammon grenade right into the tank. There was one awful explosion, smoke and fire all around the tank, and the commander... went straight up in the air like a champagne cork.'

Sgt O. B. Hill, US 82nd Abn Div (17)

'As I dove for the ditch, all hell broke loose. We had been ambushed. The German behind the hedge had his weapon set on full automatic and it sprayed bullets all over the area. Instantaneously, shots started coming from the buildings in St Côme-du-Mont and from the hedges ... It was obvious that we were badly outnumbered and that the Germans were well emplaced and planned to defend St Côme-du-Mont stubbornly. So there we were, 200 yards north of St Côme-du-Mont meeting superior fire from a major force. We had no automatic weapons, no radios, only our semiautomatic rifles and a few pistols. We hardly knew each other, but we were getting well acquainted, and we were working well together.'

Capt Sam Gibbons, 501st PIR,
US 101st Abn Div (18)

A squad of Airborne troopers probe forward down the lane beside a medieval Norman church, while one NCO cautiously watches the rear. The scattered groups of paratroopers and glider men fought many sudden encounter actions with equally confused German troops. (US Army)

'We heard the drone of aircraft and looked up to see the sky full of C-47 cargo planes towing American gliders ... The planes made one circle and started to cut loose the gliders. We watched helplessly while one glider after another attempted to land in the fields around us and crashed. When they hit something all the equipment inside tore loose and hurtled through the nose of the glider, killing or injuring the men in front of it. I doubt if 10 per cent of the gliders landing on that field did so without crashing and very few of the men who landed were in any shape to fight.'

Lt Charles E. Sammon,
2nd Bn, 505th PIR,
US 82nd Abn Div (19)

(Simon Pugh-Jones)

(Simon Pugh-Jones)

'The thing that I remember most was a soldier who had his leg blown off right by the knee and the only thing left attached was his patellar tendon. And I had him down there in this ditch and I said, "Son, I'm going to have to cut the rest of your leg off and you're back to bullet-biting time because I don't have anything to use for an anaesthetic." And he said, "Go ahead, Doc." I cut the patellar tendon and he didn't even whimper.'

Maj David Thomas, medical officer, 508th PIR, US 82nd Abn Div (20)

'We found another glider and the guys who were in it. It had one 105 howitzer and two rounds of ammunition. We put the howitzer on the road facing the direction we thought the enemy would be coming from. At dawn we met my major, who was happy to see us ... Looking around, we finally reasoned that we were on the wrong side of the church at Ste Mère-Eglise. It was June 7 before we were reunited with the rest of the guys from the HQ Battery, and 28 days before we were replaced by Inf Divs.'

Sgt George Maruschak, 328th Glider Field Arty Bn, US 82nd Abn Div (21)

'Machine-gun, artillery and small-arms fire was now coming up from barns, houses and German firing positions in scattered locations. In the glider we tried to make ourselves as small as possible, elbows close to the body, knees pulled up to the chest and head bowed down ... We came across the top of a hedgerow, knocked the wheels off the glider, crash-landed, and came to a stop about 4 miles inland from "Utah" beach, in the general vicinity of Ste Mère-Eglise and the smaller village of Chef-du-Pont.

'Miraculously, no one was hurt. As we hit the ground I felt a terrible pain in my back and thought my back was broken, but I was able to move my legs and knew I was lucky.'

Capt Harold A. Shebeck, 325th Glider Inf Regt, US 82 Abn Div (22)

'The Germans had infiltrated so well and struck so suddenly that no one knew what was going on. I managed to round up the remnants of my platoon and set up a machine gun to keep firing at the German position so they wouldn't attempt to advance further. I also got a man armed with a carbine and rifle grenades to start firing grenades into their position. The best discovery, however, was a mortar man from one of the rifle companies with a complete mortar and a supply of ammunition. In parachute drops this is a rare find, as often some vital part will be missing as a result of the drop. With grenades and mortar shells falling into their positions, the Germans had no choice but to move. They couldn't go back as we had set up a machine gun to cover their retreat. One by one they attempted to go over the top of their protective embankment into the ditch ... There were about twenty men in the position and about half of them made it into the ditch; the rest were either killed or wounded as they came out.'

Lt Charles E.Sammon, 2nd Bn, 505th PIR, US 82nd Abn Div (23)

'I landed outside Mountebourg, north of Ste Mère-Eglise, instead of at St Martin de Varreville, just in from "Utah" beach, which was our designated drop zone. We had our first action just outside Le Ham early that morning, after we had stopped and destroyed three or four German ammunition trucks. During the next three days, we were involved in several skirmishes, usually against superior numbers and weapons. We had only carbines and grenades. Out of the twelve 7.5mm howitzers in the battalion, only one was ever recovered and put into action. On about June 9 I was wounded and taken prisoner ...'

Cpl Arley Goodenkauf, 377th Parachute Field Arty Regt, US 101st Abn Div (24)

'A sight that has never left my memory ... was a picture story of the death of one 82nd Airborne trooper. He had occupied a German foxhole and made it his personal Alamo. In a half circle around the hole lay the bodies of nine German soldiers. The body closest to the hole was only three feet away, a [grenade] in its fist. The other distorted forms lay where they had fallen, testimony to the ferocity of the fight. His ammunition bandoliers were still on his shoulders, empty ... Cartridge cases littered the ground. His rifle stock was broken in two. He had fought alone and, like many others that night, he had died alone.'

Pte John E. Fitzgerald, 502nd PIR, US 101st Abn Div (25)

'When would the beach forces come? They should have already done so. Maybe the whole invasion had failed. All we knew was the situation in Chef-du-Pont, and Chef-du-Pont is a very small town.

'At 2400 hours our fears were dispelled. Reconnaissance elements of the 4th Inf Div wheeled into town. They shared their rations with us. It was D-Day plus one in Normandy. As I sat pondering the day's events, I reflected upon the details of the fighting and the bravery of every man participating in it. We had done some things badly. But overall, with a hodge-podge of troops from several units who had never trained together, didn't even know one another, engaged in their first combat, we had done okay. We captured our bridge and we held it.'

Capt Roy Creek, 507th PIR, US 82nd Abn Div (26)

(Right) A playing card emblem painted on his helmet identifies the regiment of this wounded lieutenant from the 506th PIR, 101st Abn Div being helped off an LST at Southampton, England, on 9 June.

British & Canadian Airborne

The British 6th Abn Div (incorporating a Canadian battalion) was dropped on the eastern bank of the Orne river north-east of Caen, to guard the left flank of Sword Beach. In a high wind the 3rd and 5th Parachute Bdes, like their American comrades, were confused by navigation errors, scattered drops and lost beacons, and they too lost numbers of men drowned under their huge burdens in unexpected floods. Nevertheless, they succeeded in their missions of seizing the bridges over the Orne and the parallel Caen Canal; destroying the Merville battery; blowing the bridges over the Dives to the east; and setting up a defensive position on the high ground between the two rivers, around Varaville. The very first Allied soldiers to attack the Germans in France, at about 0020 on 6 June, were Maj John Howard's D Company, Oxfordshire & Buckinghamshire Light Infantry, who captured 'Pegasus Bridge' over the Caen Canal at Benouville, and the nearby Orne river bridge, after a pinpoint glider landing. Most of the gliders of 6th Airlanding Bde, with such vehicles and heavy weapons as the division boasted, landed around Ranville later on D-Day.

All the following quotations are from officers and men of the units of British 6th Abn Div, and the squadrons of the Glider Pilot Regt and the Royal Air Force which carried them to Normandy.

'To say that one moved off to the aircraft in a smart soldier-like manner would be untrue. We all looked like pregnant ducks carrying everything but the kitchen sink ... What was I carrying? A Sten gun, which would eventually be stuffed inside the parachute harness against my chest. Webbing equipment and small pack which contained so much that I intended to jump ... with it attached by a length of strong string to the D on my parachute harness so that I could let it down after I was free of the aircraft ... and I would hopefully find it on landing ... Four Sten magazines filled with 9mm ammunition, a spare small box of 9mm, two 36 Mills grenades, one phosphorus grenade, two sticks of plastic explosive for the anti-tank [Gammon] grenade, mess tin, knife, fork, spoon, twenty-four-hour ration pack, map, message pad, entrenching tool, parachute helmet, maroon beret, mirror, bootlaces, spare socks, singlet and briefs, small towel and washing and shaving kit, pay book, handkerchiefs, writing paper, envelopes, pen, pencil, binoculars, torch, French money, field dressing, one packet (three) contraceptives, toilet paper, boiled sweets, camouflage smock, boot polish/dubbin, blanco and brush, comb, plus of course any personal items ... A bonus tucked into my smock was half a bottle of brandy which had been issued to officers and senior NCOs for medicinal purposes.'

Sgt Jack Harries, 9th Parachute Bn (1)

'We held tight and braced for landing. The usual slight bump, a small jerk, and a much heavier thump told us that the glider had made contact with the ground ... It jerked again, left the ground, bumped again, bouncing forward at high speed ... the darkness was filled with a stream of sparks caused by the skids scraping the ground ... a crash ... I was perched at an angle, peering into misty grey haze. From somewhere streams of lights ... seemed to float in gathering speed towards us ...

'Corporal Bailey and Wally Parr clambered up the canal bank and lobbed grenades through the pillbox slit. My platoon's job now was to fight our way across the bridge as quickly as possible ... Major Howard was already standing on the approach to the bridge roaring, "Come on boys, this is it." As we reached the bridge, we let fly with rifles, Sten guns and grenades. A hidden machine gun clattered into life, we returned fire and kept going, Lt Brotheridge in the lead. The enemy machine gun fired another long burst and our platoon commander fell mortally wounded. As we neared the far side the Germans scattered.'

Pte Denis Edwards, D Coy, Ox. & Bucks. Light Infantry (2)

(Left) Massively loaded paratroopers emplane on the night of 5/6 June 1944. During World War II British paratroopers were not issued reserve parachutes in chest packs — they jumped from far too low to have had any time to use them; the pronounced 'beer bellies' of some of these men are the result of extra ammunition and rations stuffed into the front of their jump smocks. Their webbing haversacks are worn beneath the smocks, below the main parachute backpacks. (IWM CH 13303)

(Below) American Waco CG-4A (left) and British Horsa gliders lined up for the airborne phase of the invasion. The Waco, made of steel tubing and fabric, had a loaded weight of 7,500lb; the Horsa, almost entirely made of timber and plywood, weighed 15,500lb loaded. They had the capacity to carry 15 and 25 men respectively, or a combination of men and equipment. Some US units used Horsas on D-Day; they could carry jeeps, anti-tank guns and other heavy weapons. (IWM CH 13290)

(Martin Brayley)

'I was [navigator] in an Albemarle towing a Horsa glider on 6th June 1944 to Caen. Prior to dropping our glider, I saw a Hamilcar [glider] about one mile in front of us carrying, as I recollect, troops on the upper deck and a tank on the lower. Suddenly the tank broke through the front of the glider plummeting to the sea, followed by the glider, which had been cast off from the towing aircraft.

'After dropping our glider we were immediately hit by anti-aircraft fire and the starboard engine and the rest of the wing outward fell off. We crash-landed at Greenham Common. The only casualty amongst the crew was the rear-gunner who was hit by shrapnel in the backside. He also had the wire connecting his parachute handle to his parachute shot through, and was most upset until I gave him my parachute. I was, you must understand, no hero, as we flew all the way back to England at about 100 feet and in as straight a line as possible, so a parachute was superfluous.'

**Warrant Officer F .J. Parslow,
No 296 Sqn RAF (3)**

'We took off at about midnight. I was up front behind the pilots. We had six sappers whose job was to blow the guns. Over the Battery we were hit by light anti-aircraft fire. One shell hit the flamethrower. The glider and the unfortunate chap were on fire for the last few seconds of the approach. As we swooped in we saw the Battery. We lifted over a wire fence which we thought was outside the Battery, and crash-landed in an orchard about 150 yards away. As we all rushed out, except for the poor chap on fire, we heard shooting, which we realised was the Battalion in the Battery.

'We heard noises in the opposite direction, and realised they must be Germans coming up a narrow lane. We jumped into the ditch and engaged them. After a while as it was getting light, the firing died down. I heard a shout behind us, and there coming through a minefield was the Battalion Physical Training Instructor. We shouted, "Go back. It's a minefield." "No it's not, it's a dummy, you're to rejoin the Battalion," he replied. This was our first contact with our Battalion'.

**Lt Hugh Pond, 9th Parachute Bn,
detached for glider-borne
attack on Merville Battery(4)**

'We were carrying 20 paratroopers and an Alsatian dog trained to jump from the back of a lorry. On a temporary rack fitted on the belly we carried a number of small anti-personnel bombs to drop as we crossed the Normandy beaches [to] encourage the defenders to keep their heads down. Shortly before we made landfall something exploded on the land right ahead. A vast sheet of yellow flame lit up the sky for a second or two and in that light I saw a line of aeroplanes all going the same way, all at the same height, and I was in this mad game of follow-the-leader. I felt the slip-stream of other aeroplanes from time to time but once that rather shattering fire had died down never actually saw another. I was sure it was one of our lot that had bought it, though I was later told it was a Stirling.'

**Flt Lt P. M. Bristow,
No 575 Sqn RAF (5)**

(Left) Although the Douglas C-47 ('Skytrain' to the GIs, 'Dakota' to the British) was the workhorse of the Airborne forces, carrying most of the paratroopers and also towing gliders, many obsolescent British bomber types such as the Albemarle, Stirling and Halifax were also converted for these roles. The four-engined Stirling could carry from 20 to 24 paratroops depending on the number of equipment containers also loaded. (IWM CH 13304)

(Martin Brayley)

'When we got near the dropping zone it was a case of "Red light on; hook up; get ready to jump." The engines throttled back and it was green light on, "Go", and we were out and floating down towards France. It was so silent, only the noises of the plane's engines going away from us. Where was the war? Where were the Germans? Then I looked down ... Where was the land?

'All I could see below me was water. I panicked and set off the air-levers on my Mae West jacket under my parachute harness. Suddenly there was I, being dragged over the water by my parachute, unable to release myself from the harness. Luckily one of my section was close by and he waded over and cut me free. I was then able to stand up in waist-high water. We had landed in the flooded Dives valley.'

Pte Bill Elvin, 7th Parachute Bn (6)

'I had landed ... in the center of a field ... and thought I heard voices. "English or German?" Three figures emerged through the hedge on the south side ... muttering together, but strain as I might I could not make out one syllable of their conversation. Then ... a breeze brought me their scent ... a cross between the plastecine we used at school and a new cheap brand of scented soap. They may have seen the flash of my arm as it described an arc in their general direction to release the 36 grenade which I dared not hold any longer since the fuse had been struck for at least a second already. In fact I believe it never reached the ground before it exploded. I didn't wait to see the result, but on the explosion I was up and running like a hare in the direction I judged north-west to be. After about a minute I pulled up, partly through want of breath but also, having managed to subdue my feeling of panic, to say to myself aloud, I believe, "You ****ing brave paratrooper."'

Capt A. R. Clark, 13th Parachute Bn (7)

'I flew in a Stirling ... I remember the floor hatch being opened and seeing the surf of the coast of France. From the exit to the ground seemed only a short time as I think we were dropped from 500 feet. I had no idea where I was and was convinced I'd been dropped in the wrong place. I gathered some men and heard a vehicle. Just as we were about to open fire we realized they were English ... two RN signallers who had dropped with us to work wireless ... [for naval] artillery support. They said that in the Navy they had not been taught how to march and so they'd knocked off the Germans in the Volkswagen and were driving to the DZ.

'Our intelligence officer ... agreed we were lost. We [found] a signpost and I told him that as there were no umpires on this exercise we could cheat. He got on my shoulders and ... ran a torch along it. At that moment we heard a hunting horn which was our rallying signal and made our way to the quarry which was our RV.'

Capt G. T. Radmore, Royal Signals, 5th Parachute Bde (8)

(Martin Brayley)

Hamilcar heavy gliders landing at Ranville, 6 June. The massive Hamilcar, with a payload of nearly eight tons, could carry a light reconnaissance tank, two Bren carriers, a 25-pounder field gun, or a variety of other equipment; it needed a four-engined bomber to tow it. Inadequate restraints or simply the landing shock could cause such heavy items to break free inside the flimsy structure, with catastrophic results. (IWM B5198)

'I could see out the door of the aircraft; flashes of explosions, and a succession of bright balls of lights coming towards us: flak. One shell exploded outside the door, and the pilot took avoiding action. The stick was flung into chaos, grabbing and clutching each other in the darkness. The despatcher tapped Captain Johnson on the shoulder, the green light went on, someone shouted "Stop". The light turned red, and green again. Out went the two in front, I followed. I released my kit-bag, containing plasma. I could see a white line below, and was convinced this was a road near Varaville, marked on our map. Just as I thought everything was going to plan, I landed flat on my back in water, in a lake. I stood up, absolutely soaked ... After a few yards, [we] went straight into a six-foot ditch ... The whole place was intersected with these ditches, about 100 yards apart. It was a nightmarish, exhausting wallow, particularly falling into the ditches, because you got no warning.'

Pte James Bramwell, 224 Parachute Field Ambulance (9)

'From 500 feet, our tug descended down to the sea ... and we raced across the Channel at 130mph to keep below German radar. The black paint on our faces had become streaked with sweat. Glider pilots become fighting soldiers on landing, and flying a glider wearing Army uniform plus revolvers, rifles, pockets stuffed with hand grenades, can become a very warm business ...

'Pretty lights floated up to us ... Black puffs of smoke formed around us, but did not give us any impression of being dangerous ...

'The tow release lever was pulled ... a slow-descending half-turn brought us into line with our intended landing position. What was waiting for us? Was it the right field? ... "Hold tight," I shouted, and as we touched the ground the tip of the starboard wing struck a pole. We slewed round ... and came to a full stop ... There was a crash somewhere behind, a sound of rending wood ... another glider had collided with our tail, wrenching it almost off — just where we would have to take it off to get the jeep out. This saved us a good ten minutes ...

'A heavy Hamilcar came in very steeply ... a tank shot out of the nose ... followed by the glider helplessly out of control. It crashed somewhere in the field ... A few of the gliders were burning, their ammunition stores exploding. One could not absorb everything, except to carry out your own orders and ignore the seemingly chaotic background to it all.'

Sgt B. A. Tomblin, Glider Pilot Regt (10)

'Our drop was set for 0030 hrs ... "We are approaching the coast of France", and suddenly our aircraft was sent into turmoil with German anti-aircraft fire ... We were hurled from port to starboard ... A voice shouted, "Stand by the doors — Get ready! Red light ... Green light ... GO!" ... As I jumped I could see the amber glow from shells exploding around the aircraft. After a disastrous exit I floated down to the best landing I had ever made.

'About a hundred yards further on a group of about six men, including Lieutenant Mike Dowling of B Company, were lying in a patch of stinging nettles trying to find their bearings. We moved along a narrow road when suddenly the noise of a lorry was heard. It was full of Germans so we laid low. When the lorry had disappeared we crossed the road to be greeted by a Pathfinder, and we joined the few men who had arrived at the rendezvous. The final number reached 150.'

Pte S. F. Capon, 12th Parachute Bn (11)

'We could feel when our glider became detached from the towing plane and began to descend. As we landed with a bump we heard two or three shots fired ... We stormed out of the gliders and I well remember my amazement that the spot at which we landed looked exactly as we were told to expect. We had been given descriptions and been shown photos; there were

'About thirty Hamilcar [gliders] took off, most of them carrying Tetrarch tanks [and] crews of the Light Reconnaissance Squadron ... My memory is of an uneventful trip, and I was greatly impressed [by] the swarms of Mustang fighters escorting us across the Channel and by the sight of the Royal Navy firing broadsides into the German defences on the coast of Normandy.

'Our landing was, however, more tricky; there was a certain amount of ... tracers coming up at us, and the field in which we landed near Ranville had got telegraph poles erected to hinder the landings. We came in rather fast with our wings hitting the odd telegraph pole. A Tetrarch [drove] ... at right angles to our landing path. The tank commander ... leaped ... a second or two before we hit it at a speed of 90 to 100mph. The first pilot ... and I [discovered] the Hamilcar cockpit ... 15 to 20 feet above the ground ... the tank upside down underneath us, with grenades and cannon shells dropping ... into the field, and a strong smell of petrol ... One or two gliders nearby [were] burning fiercely as they had been mortared by the Germans.'

**S/Sgt G. H. Heaton,
Glider Pilot Regt**
(14)

biggish trees and we had to assemble near one of these, and there it really was. At that moment I admired the efficiency of all the arrangements, but from then onwards it all became very much a shambles.'
Tpr W. W. Brown, Armd Recon Regt
(12)

'We landed near Ranville and what is now Pegasus Bridge in the second wave. We found the glider with our jeep and trailer and started out for Longueval and our rendezvous. There were soldiers everywhere and, quite frankly, we were all like a herd of sheep.

'Our main problem was the snipers. We were right in their line. Close by was an officer manning a machine gun. He was wounded later and I was one of those who had to go and get him in. All those around him had been killed, picked off by the snipers. There was a wood nearby, giving them really good cover and they came in after dark, moving from tree to tree, well camouflaged. The only way to bring them down was to aim carefully directly at them, which one of our corporals did — shooting a sniper right through the forehead. The sniper was, like us, only about twenty-three or twenty-four.'

(Martin Brayley)

Unloading a jeep and trailer from a Horsa at Ranville, 6 June. The great weakness of airborne troops was their relative lack of vehicles and anti-tank guns; until the seaborne invasion force could link up with them on the objectives they had seized, they had little mobility and very little defence against armoured counter-attacks.
(IWM B5200)

'There was still some action in Ranville, and we managed to get our [anti-tank] gun to it, and were dug in and camouflaged by about 2am on 6 June ... We encountered a Frenchman at daybreak on a bike with a long loaf of bread under his arm. When he saw my 2nd Pilot and I, with black faces and helmets, he thought we were Germans and started to pull out his pass ... I spoke the little bit of French I knew — "Je suis Anglais" — and he nearly died of fright and rushed away ...

'I had been watching the skyline area towards Caen, from where we were expecting the enemy armour ... and eventually the enemy tanks and half-tracks crossed into our right angle of anti-tank guns, with infantry extended in front of them. ... All the guns opened up, and in a short time all the armoured vehicles were blown up or on fire. I feel sure that the enemy had no idea that we had that sort of anti-tank defence on the ground from the night landing, and I think it must have made the Germans delay sending more armour in, thus giving us a chance to secure the bridges. After we attacked the infantry with our Brens the enemy withdrew, but later ... gave us a pounding with mortars.'

S/Sgt Bill Higgs, Glider Pilot Regt (15)

'As the wind dispersed the early-morning mist, I could see a faint line in the distance, which resolved itself into the Normandy coast. It was 0500 hrs and we were a mere 1,200 yards from the beaches. I knew we were caught on the coastal strip being prepared for the seaborne invasion, and could see the flashes of gunfire from the distant warships. Following this came the roar of aircraft, bombs showered in astride and behind us.

'The entire coastline was blotted out by clouds of smoke and we scratched pitiful little holes in the earth. Five minutes after the bomb line passed inland a new terror threatened. Low-flying fighters strafed our area. One of the men had a bullet pass through the stock of his rifle as he held it between his hands. Branches were cut down all around us, yet we survived.'

Capt John Madden, 1st Canadian Para Bn, British 6th Abn Div (16)

'[It was] five days of the hardest fighting I had seen in the war. A narrow road ran along a ridge. We had to hold this ridge at all costs. If the Germans [346th Inf Div] had secured it, the bridgehead at Ranville would have been untenable. Involved in the fighting were the 9th Parachute Battalion, 1st Canadian Parachute Battalion and 5th Battalion Black Watch. Imagine what it

British Airborne troops pose for a photographer after the link-up, in one of many Normandy fields which were carpeted with more or less wrecked gliders. This was a 'use once and throw away' item; although gliders had loading doors, hinged nose sections or disconnecting tails, the priority after landing was to get the load out by any means to hand, and few survived landing and unloading in a recoverable state. It should also be remembered that of 355 British gliders used, 100 of the pilots became casualties. (IWM B5349)

was like for a 9th Battalion soldier. They had never seen a shot fired in anger until 48 hours before. Their average age was 20. They had suffered an appalling night drop on D-Day. They had stormed the Merville Battery and attacked Le Plein. They arrived on the ridge at midnight on 7th June, 90 strong, having set off from England with over 600 officers and soldiers. They were minus most of their equipment, and not exactly fresh.

'In the first eight days ... my Brigade, which started around 2,000 strong, lost 50 officers and 1,000 other ranks.'

Brig James Hill, OC 3rd Parachute Bde (17)

Getting There By Sea
The Crossing

The basic plan for the amphibious landings involved five beaches in two main sectors, the US to the west astride the estuary of the Vire river, and the British/Canadian to the east between Arromanches and Ouistreham at the mouth of the Orne. Many factors had been taken into consideration, and the separation of the beaches was accepted as the least of several possible evils.

The defences the assault troops faced were basically static, and had no depth. Forced to defend the entire coastline with weak forces, Field Marshal Rommel had overseen the construction of a system of strong concrete gun emplacements and bunkers, surrounded with entrenchments for infantry defence, along the top of beaches which were protected by deep belts of obstacles and sown with millions of mines. Elements of five German infantry divisions held these defences (the 91st, 243rd, 352nd, 709th and 716th); but these were mostly of poor quality, and so weak in vehicles and heavy weapons that once dislodged from their bunkers they had little potential for manoeuvre or counter-attack.

The Western Naval Task Force of 931 ships transported the assault troops and equipment for the two US beaches; the Eastern Naval Task Force of 1,796 ships set sail for the three British and Canadian beaches. Altogether the Allied armada totalled 2,727 ships carrying 2,606 landing craft — 5,333 vessels in all, including 137 warships which would provide naval gunfire bombardment. This, the greatest fleet in history, carried 176,475 men and 21,651 vehicles.

The last-minute postponement of the landings from 5 to 6 June, caused by bad weather, meant that thousands of troops who had already embarked on 3 and 4 June had to spend up to three days and nights aboard. The cramped conditions and sometimes rough seas made this a memorable ordeal for many. Other GIs and Tommies made the best of their enforced leisure, trying to take their minds off the coming test; many recall feeling confident about the overall operation, but anxious lest they personally should let their comrades down. For the US 29th and British 3rd Divisions, destined for the first assault waves at Omaha and Gold Beaches, this would be their first taste of battle. (US National Archives)

Photographer Robert Capa, aboard the USS *Chase*, divided the GIs into three types:

'... The planners, the gamblers and the writers of last letters. The gamblers were to be found on the upper deck, clustering around a pair of tiny dice and putting thousands of dollars on the blanket. The last-letter writers hid in corners and put down beautiful sentences on paper leaving their favourite shotguns to kid brothers and their dough to the family. As for the planners, they were down in the gymnasium in the bottom of the ship, lying on their stomachs around a rubber carpet on which was placed a miniature of every house and tree on the French coast. The platoon leaders picked their way between the rubber villages and looked for protection behind the rubber trees and in the rubber ditches on the mattress.' (1)

'When we boarded the ship the weather looked so bad we wondered if it would ever clear up and whether the whole thing would be called off ... We played cards, relaxed as much as possible, thought about our families and prayed ... We would try to play different games, to entertain ourselves and get our minds off the real objective, but we would drift back into quietness, more or less thinking about our homes and things like that.

'Quite a few boys wrote letters and gave them to friends to send home or see that their parents got them. They were farewell letters. Some boys said that they knew they'd never make it ... I did more praying during that period of time than I think I've ever done in my life ... I wasn't yellow, but I was scared, no question about it. I was scared to death.'

Pfc Robert Koch, 1st Bn, 116th Inf Regt, US 29th Inf Div (2)

'...In the back of one's mind one rather looked forward to it. Don't forget, we were a very, very good regiment ... It was a family concern and we had some very good chaps. I had the highest possible opinion of the morale ...

'On the crossing I remember going up on deck with the captain and looking in front of us and there was nothing! Absolutely nothing, just sea. Then I can remember looking behind me and seeing the place absolutely solid with pinpoint lights; it was the most extraordinary feeling. It looked as if one was at the centre of the most enormous armada and the sensation was really very dramatic ...

'I wasn't sick at all; I was surprised that I wasn't, but I wasn't. I got a little sleep. I interfered with the chaps as little as possible. I went back down to find out if they were all right, had had their grub, that the tanks were secure .. half of them were asleep and the other half very dozy, so I left them alone.'

Capt Robert Neave, 13th/18th Royal Hussars, British 27th Armd Bde (3)

'The wind howled and it rained in vicious scuds. The skipper said in his speech: "The High Command must be counting heavily on surprise, for the Germans must surely think that not even Englishmen could be fools enough to start an invasion on a night like this."

'Feeling small, I set about my final packing. I spliced my identity discs on new string and gloomily hung them round my neck. I dished out sea-sick tablets and morphine and talked to all the troops on final medical plans. I had a heated tussle with the brigade major on the subject of the rum issue, finally settling that the troops could have it thirty minutes before landing and not prior to getting into the

LCAs [Landing Craft Assault]. With cold and sea-sickness ahead, this would have been folly.'

Capt J. H. Patterson, medical officer, 4 Cdo, British 1st Special Service Bde (4)

'[Seasickness] capsules had been issued to us with our battle kits. Well, we took the first two and they almost killed us. The capsules had a strong sleeping powder in them, and by noon we were in a drugged stupor ... They constricted our throats, made our mouths bone dry and dilated the pupils of our eyes until we could hardly see'.

War correspondent Ernie Pyle, with the US 29th Inf Div (5)

'The sea seemed to be getting rougher and our craft began to toss and roll so much that it was all we could do to keep on our feet. The lads seemed to have quietened down somewhat. Many of them, including the sergeant major and the skipper, were old campaigners and probably knew what we were going to run into.

'[We] got down on the floor to have a sleep, covering ourselves with our blankets, but our sleep was very broken because the storm grew worse and we were thrown all over the place ... to make matters worse we now began to have terrible headaches owing to the pills we had taken ... We felt that bad, we began to wish we were dead and I do not think any of us really worried about the coming events.'

L/Bdr C. Morris, 6 Cdo, British 1st Special Service Bde (6)

Sherman tanks of the British 13th/18th Royal Hussars, 27th Armoured Brigade crossing the Channel. The forward tanks are Duplex Drive (DD) or 'swimming' tanks, with added collapsible canvas skirts, sealed hulls and tall exhaust housings. These were intended to spearhead the landings on all five beaches, but many were launched too far out and in water too rough to survive. The great majority of those launched off Omaha sank; in this case the crews' lives depended on getting out instantly and taking to rubber dinghies — which many failed to do. At Utah the DD tanks mostly performed satisfactorily; at the British and Canadian beaches the rough seas led to a decision not to launch most of the DDs, and they were landed straight onto the beaches. (IWM B5110)

A number of vessels in the invasion armada were crewed by the **US Coast Guard** — this Landing Ship Infantry (LSI) is one. These GIs wear full equipment and inflatable lifebelts, and carry their weapons in clear pliofilm bags; even so, when they hit the beach many soldiers would soon find them jammed by wet sand. The black cardboard tubes stuck under the web equipment carry mortar or bazooka ammunition. In the background are barrage balloons, towed by the ships on steel cables to deter low-level air attack. (US National Archives)

The lifebelt was inflated by triggering small carbon dioxide canisters. Supposed to be inflated only at the last minute in an emergency, it was worn awkwardly, under the personal equipment, and usually too low for safety — a heavily-loaded soldier's centre of gravity was too low, and the waves might easily up-end him to drown helplessly. Many men were pitched into the sea when their landing craft were sunk by artillery well off shore, or when the ramps were lowered too far from the beach. A significant number of the D-Day fatalities were due to drowning rather than enemy fire. (US National Archives)

248431

In the dawn of 6 June 1944, Landing Craft Vehicles/Personnel (LCVPs) hit Omaha Beach and disembark their infantry in choppy, waist-deep water. The haze of aerial and naval bombardment hangs over the beach and the high ground beyond; but at Omaha this had done very little damage to the strong German defensive positions. On all the beaches the dust and smoke of the initial bombardment hampered spotter planes from correcting the fall of shot, contributing to the disappointing results. (US National Archives)

'The hour came round and we all went up in a single file to the upper deck and so out through the double blackout curtains to the main deck ... Promptly at four o'clock the transport stopped engines and we all clambered over the iron railings into the landing craft which hung from the side of the ship ...

'We hit the Channel with a thud and away we went ... As we went in toward the beach we could see the colored flares that the amphibious engineers had placed. As we passed the last flare, the battleship Texas fired ... Rocket barges gave us our first real fright. They started to fire their huge banks of rockets ... on the upward roll, so [the rockets] dropped a few hundred yards in front of us, still a good two miles offshore ... By this time some of the guys were seasick and some were arguing over little things that didn't count. Some guys, like myself, were just standing there in the boat, thinking and shivering.'

Cpl Gilbert G. Murdoch, 1st Bn, 116th Inf Regt, US 29th Inf Div (7)

'We were also cautioned to loosen our helmet straps as if we lost our grip on the rope ladders going down the side of the ship, we could plunge down with force enough to break our necks when the water hit the helmet rim. So I made sure I had a good grip. Better some battered knuckles than drowning.'

Pte Bruce Bradley, 29th Field Arty Bn, US 4th Inf Div (8)

'We were all assembled with the troops on our various landing craft still hanging from davits on the side of the [SS Empire Broadsword]. They hung in tiers, one row above the other. The chaplain said a few words and blessed us after which the first tier started to lower away ... the waves must have been twenty feet high.

'We hit the crest of a wave and I started to take off the forward hook ... unfortunately my stern sheetsman ...couldn't release his because by that time we had dropped into a trough and the cable had gone taught. Consequently we were hanging by the stern hook and all the troops ... fell forward all on top of one another ... When the next wave brought us up level we managed to release the stern hook, at which time we dropped with an almighty splash in the drink ...

'Previous to being lowered away we had all been issued with a hay box of stew to give the troops a hot meal. After we had been travelling for about two or three miles I decided to see if the troops would like anything to eat ... as soon as the troops smelled it and saw it the majority were sick on the spot ... '

Royal Marine Derek Pratt, LCA coxswain (9)

'We just lowered the [LCT's] ramp and drove the DUKW down into the ocean. We had to circle ... waiting for the time to go. We lost half the DUKWs in the rough seas while awaiting the signal. [They] would ride up a swell and instead of coming back down it would go into it, and go under. They just shipped water, turned over sideways and sunk.

'... I remember the battleship Texas firing broadsides into shore while we were close by. It was God-awful, terrible explosions — muzzle blast in our ears ... the smoke ring passed by us and it looked like a funnel of a tornado, growing larger and larger and finally dissipating ... I don't believe we should have been that close because we actually felt the muzzle blast ....

'All the ships did a great job except the LCT rocket ships which didn't get close enough to hit their targets. Destroyers came within a thousand yards of the shore and let go their five- and six-inch guns ... The flash of the big guns was blinding and the explosions from the muzzles were deafening.'

S/Sgt William H. Lewis, 1st Bn, 116th Inf Regt, US 29th Inf Div (10)

'Blowing spume had soaked us before we hit the Channel. It seemed we would surely swamp, and life belts were inflated, not only on our persons but on reels of telephone wire, radios and demolition packs, in the hope that if they were lost in the surf they would float ashore. The expansion of perhaps a hundred belts added to the bulk already crowding the craft, and so we rode, packed in an open can, feet awash in water and altogether cold, wet and miserable.'

Lt Charles Cawthon, 2nd Bn, 116th Inf Regt, US 29th Inf Div (11)

'We were twelve miles off shore as we climbed into our seat assignments on the LCAs and lowered by davits to the extremely heavy sea ... Prior to loading, friends said their goodbyes and good luck ... The feeling among most of the men was that the landing would be a 'walk-in' affair, but that later we could expect stiff counter-attacks. This didn't worry us too much because by then tanks, heavy artillery and air support would bolster our defense ...

'The Channel was extremely rough and it wasn't long before we had to help the craft's pumps by baling water with our helmets. The cold spray blew in and soon we were soaked. I used a gas cape as shelter from the spray. Lack of oxygen under the [cape] caused seasickness ... My thinking, as we approached the beach, was that if the boat didn't hurry up and get us in I would die from seasickness ... At this point, death is not so dreadful. I didn't care what the Germans had to offer, I had to set foot on dry land.'

Sgt John R. Slaughter, 1st Bn, 116th Inf Regt, US 29th Inf Div (12)

The American Beaches

To the west, Utah Beach was on the east-facing coast of the Cotentin Peninsula, extending roughly a mile and a half each side of La Madeleine. The assault here would be led by the 4th Inf Div, supported by amphibious tanks, combat engineers to clear the countless beach obstacles and mines laid along Hitler's boasted 'Atlantic Wall', and many other specialist units. Once they had fought their way ashore and the specialists had cleared paths inland the assault troops would be followed by the 90th Division.

Omaha Beach was about 11 miles east of Utah, on the other side of the Vire estuary. It was about 4 miles long, roughly bounded by Vierville and Colleville, and unlike all the other beaches it was backed by tall bluffs with cliffs at each end. The assault troops would be from the 1st and 29th Inf Divs, with the usual specialist assistance, and from the 5th and 2nd Rangers; the latter would seize a commanding battery at Pointe-du-Hoc. Once Omaha was secure the 1st and 29th Inf Divs were to be reinforced by the 2nd Inf Division.

While the various assault units contained many individuals with battle experience in the Mediterranean or elsewhere, of the main divisions only the 1st — the 'Big Red One' — had seen combat before as a formation, in French North Africa, Tunisia and Sicily.

Both beaches were targeted for a massive preliminary bombardment by aircraft and naval gunfire, to destroy the German gun emplacements, shatter the defenders' will to resist, and blow craters all over the beaches as foxholes for the attackers.

★ ★ ★

In the event, the landings at Utah were remarkably successful. Unexpectedly high winds and tide, and the loss of guide boats, pushed the whole assault force nearly a mile south of their planned landfall — to a point where the defences were actually weaker. The preliminary air and naval bombardment had done its job effectively. Though slower than planned, most of the amphibious DD tanks did eventually get ashore and, with tanks landed straight onto the beach, supported the infantry assaults on the badly shaken defenders, while tank-dozers helped clear gaps in the seawall. Gen Theodore Roosevelt Jr. (son of the for-

mer president, and a veteran of the 'Big Red One') took the initiative to drive straight inland rather than trying to find the planned landing sites. Despite continuing artillery fire on what soon became a terribly congested beach, the casualties were lower then anyone had dared dream.

It was on Omaha Beach that the US Army suffered its most costly setbacks, and 'Bloody Omaha' became a name to set beside Tarawa Atoll in the roll of American military sacrifices.

The landing craft were lowered about 12 miles out, beyond the range of enemy guns; but in the choppy sea many foundered and took their heavily-laden soldiers to the bottom. Most of the DD tanks sank, only five struggling ashore. The air bombardment, hampered by cloud, missed its targets, and the preliminary naval gunfire was much less accurate and effective than hoped (though later several US Navy destroyers came right inshore and provided heroic support). The barrages of rockets from specially modified landing craft fell short. Many landing craft were hit by German artillery while still well off the beach, and others were wrecked by obstacles and mines. From H-hour, 0630, the first wave of infantry — and their accompanying engineers, briefed to clear the beach obstacles for the following waves — were simply massacred. Wrecked craft at the waterline obstructed those coming behind; many of the few tanks which got ashore were soon knocked out. By about 0830, with no exits captured and the tide coming in, the narrowing beach was so congested with casualties and disorganised men cowering in the illusory shelter of the low seawall under artillery, mortar, and direct machine gun fire that all further landings were postponed. Absolute failure seemed imminent.

By mid-morning some movement was being achieved, however. Heroic junior officers and NCOs — some of them inspired by the example of commanders like Colonel George Taylor of the 1st Div's 16th Inf Regt, and General Norman Cota, assistant commander of the 29th Div — managed to get their surviving men moving, and started to shoot and blast themselves ways off the beach. One by one the machine gun posts and pillboxes were silenced. Shelling continued for most of the day, but by mid-afternoon several vehicle

exits had been opened off the beach and troops were moving inland in increasing numbers.

UTAH

'We were about the first craft in, and the enemy fire was light until they found out what was going on. We reached the beach with Brigadier-General Theodore Roosevelt Jnr., and he told us not to lay there but to move in off the beach. We had never been under fire before and he walked from soldier to soldier and told us to move. We attacked some pill-boxes and I spent 55 days treating the wounded. I was then hit myself and shipped back to England to recover.'

Pte Calvin Grose, 22nd Inf Regt, US 4th Inf Div (1)

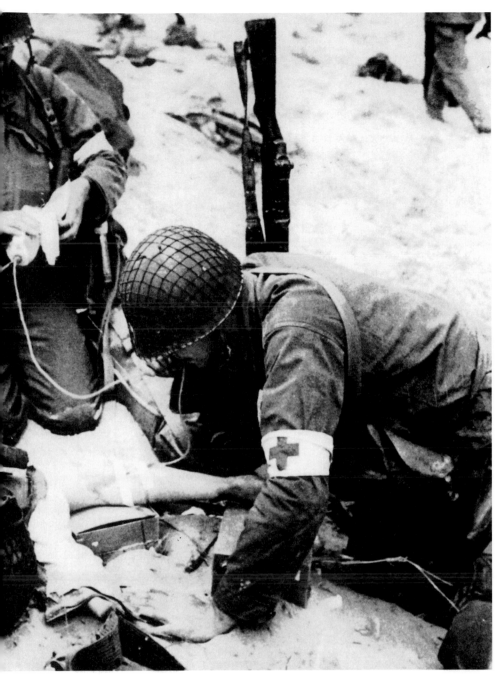

US 4th Inf Div medics treating one of their own on Utah Beach. Riflemen were strictly forbidden to stop and help a fallen comrade, beyond applying his own field dressing; they usually stuck his rifle upright in the ground to mark his position for the medics following the advance. The 4th Inf Div suffered only some 200 casualties on D-Day, mostly to mines — far less than it had lost in Operation 'Tiger' off Slapton Sands in late April. (US

(Tim Hawkins)

(Tim Hawkins)

'My position was in the right rear of the boat and I could hear the bullets splitting the air over our heads and I looked back and all I could see was two hands on the wheel and a hand on each .50-caliber machine gun, which the Navy guys were firing. I said to my platoon leader, Lieutenant Rebarchek, "These guys aren't even looking where they are going or shooting." About that time the coxswain stood up and looked at the beach and then ducked back down ... we just prayed they would get us on the beach ...

'I jumped out in waist-deep water. We had 200 feet to go to shore and you couldn't run, you could just kind of push forward. We finally made it to the edge of the water, then we had 200 yards of open beach to cross, through the obstacles. But fortunately most of the Germans were not able to fight, they were all shook up from the bombing and the shelling and the rockets and most of them just wanted to surrender.'

Sgt Malvin Pike, 2nd Bn, 8th Inf Regt, US 4th Inf Div (2)

After the heavy losses of Operation 'Tiger' in April the plans for D-Day were modified to provide rescue boats following the landing craft in. These men being saved by the crew of a Coast Guard cutter seem to wear Navy lifejackets.
(US National Archives)

'Those were the first men inland, and suddenly they started stepping on mines, S-mines, Bouncing Betties. These mines bounced up and exploded. These men began screaming and running back to the beach with the blood just flowing. And that's when the tanks started in.'

Sgt Vincent Powell, US 237th Engineer Combat Bn (3)

'As we approached the shore we got down as low as possible in the tanks, and as the ramp dropped and we went into the water, our tank was hit with artillery at least three times. One shell hit right by my ear and cracked the side of the tank about a foot long. I still have a loss of hearing because of that.

'Captain Warren was calling for someone to help him pull a jeep from the water, and three sergeants ran to help him.

Donald Schlemmer and I got off the tank, ran to the concrete wall, and got into a fox-hole, when we heard a shell coming. When the smoke, sand and water had cleared, the three sergeants lay there dead, and Captain Warren had a piece of shrapnel in his hand. We backed the tank to the edge of the water and pulled the jeep onshore, and then we did the same thing with a half-track jamming an opening in the sea wall, pulling it out of the way. Then we went through the wall into a field, where our tank went into a shell hole and tore off a track.'

Walter Schaad, US tank bn (4)

'By middle afternoon the beach had changed from nothing but obstacles to a small city. It was apparent that we NCD units had done our job well because as far as I could see to one side the beach was all the way opened, there was nothing holding the landing craft back. We figured our day was well spent, even though no one ever knew who we were ... The coxswains didn't like us because we always had so many explosives with us. When we were inland, the Army officers wanted to know what is the Navy doing in here.'

Sgt Orval Wakefield, US Navy construction/demolition bn (5)

OMAHA

'The cutter ... saw a stricken LCT which was slowly capsizing as it sank. On the decks over thirty men were trapped, including a wounded man with nearly severed legs ... We threw heaving lines to men in the water. Two or three of them were screaming, "Oh, save me ... I'm hurt bad ... please, please, please!" and I yelled back, "Hang on, Mac, we're coming" ... We needed ten pairs of hands more ... A member of the cutter's crew jumped over the side to help the man with the injured legs ... we had a hell of a time getting him aboard because his clothing was waterlogged and he was weighted down with helmet, rifle, pack, ammunition ...

'I watched one man from the bow. He shouted, "I can't stay up, I can't stay up." And he didn't. I couldn't reach him with a heaving line and when we came towards him his head was in the water ... No more than two minutes after we had picked up the rest of them, the burning ship turned turtle and disappeared from sight.'

War correspondent Carter Barber, on US Coast Guard rescue cutter (6)

(Tim Hawkins)

An LCVP set alight by enemy fire approaches Omaha Beach. The thick line of obstacles can be seen along the edge of the water. (US National Archives)

'The cliff-like ridge was covered with well-concealed foxholes and many semi-permanent bunkers. The bunkers were practically unnoticeable from the front. Their firing openings were toward the flank so that they could bring flanking crossfire to the beach as well as all the way up the slope of the bluff. The bunkers had diagrams of fields of fire, and these were framed under glass and mounted on the walls beside the firing platforms...

'I took a look toward the shore and my heart took a dive. I couldn't believe how peaceful, how untouched, and how tranquil the scene was. The terrain was green. All buildings and houses were intact. The church steeples were proudly and defiantly standing in place. "Where," I yelled to no one in particular, "is the damned Air Corps?"'

Capt Robert Walker, HQ Co, 116th Inf Regt, US 29th Inf Div (7)

A line of dead GIs already lie along the water's edge as infantry wade ashore from an LCVP on Omaha. (US National Archives)

'We were so confident ... that on the way in most of my men and I were sitting on top of the engine room decking of the landing craft, enjoying the show, fascinated by the barrage from the rocket ships. About one thousand rockets shattered the beach directly where we were to land. It looked pretty good ...

'We hit the sandbar, dropped the ramp, and then all hell poured loose on us. The soldiers in the boat received a hail of machine-gun bullets. The Army lieutenant was immediately killed, shot through the head.'

Chief Electrician's Mate Alfred Sears, US Navy (8)

'When the ramp went down on the boat, I knew we were in trouble. The first thing I heard was like a woodpecker pecking on a tree. It was bullets rattling against the ramp of the boat and then big plumes of smoke went up and I saw that Lieutenant Fitzsimmons — who was a good friend of mine — his landing craft was hit by an 88 or a mortar right on the ramp, and it just blew up, and I thought, "There goes 1 Platoon" ...

'When the ramp dropped we went down and the water was ice-cold. We had these big packs on, we were carrying three days' rations — not that the Rangers carry much, only D-rations, little chocolate bars — and we were carrying ammunition and grenades and all these things along with a gas mask — which we never did need, fortunately. A lot of the men were wearing lifebelts ... but I think that most of our people were smart enough not to inflate them, because if you are wearing an inflated life-jacket when the waves hit you, you turn upside down in the water and drown.'

Lt Robert Edlin, US 2nd Ranger Bn (9)

'I went up about, I don't know, forty, fifty feet. The rope was wet and kind of muddy. My hands just couldn't hold, they were like grease, and I came sliding back down. As I was going down, I wrapped my foot around the rope and slowed myself up as much as I could, but still I burned my hands. If the rope hadn't been so wet I wouldn't have been able to hang on for the burning.

'I landed right beside Sweeney there, and he says, "What's the matter, Sundby — chicken? Let me — I'll show you how to climb." So he went up first and I was right up after him, and when I got to the top, Sweeney says, "Hey, Sundby, don't forget to zig-zag."'

Pte Sigurd Sundby, US 2nd Ranger Bn at Pointe-du-Hoc (10)

(Above) As they struggled ashore the assault waves of the 29th and 1st Inf Divs, the 2nd and 5th Ranger Bns and the combat engineer units were completely dominated by German firing positions in the face of and at the top of the bluffs overlooking the beach. At the base of the bluffs there were twelve artillery strongpoints sited to enfilade the beach from end to end, mounting guns of up to 88mm and 105mm calibre in sideways-facing embrasures shielded from the seaward side. (US National Archives)

(Left) At Pointe-du-Hoc, about 4½ miles west of Omaha, three companies of the 2nd Ranger Bn were tasked with climbing the 120-foot cliffs and attacking a battery of five 155mm guns which threatened both American beaches. The timetable went wrong; many men were lost simply landing and reaching the base of the cliff; special equipment failed; but the Rangers climbed the cliff anyway, partly thanks to supporting fire from a destroyer. They fought their way into the battery only to find that the heavy guns had been removed; but they were located inland and disabled later that morning. Despite the heavy casualties at Pointe-du-Hoc, it was in fact the

three companies landed on Omaha which took the worst losses: C Co lost 21 killed (out of about 65), and Lt Sidney Salomon recalls: "I had 37 men in my LCA, and when I got to the top [of the bluff] I had nine."

'It was now apparent that we were coming ashore in one of the carefully registered killing zones of German machine-guns and mortars. The havoc they had wrought was all around in an incredible chaos — bodies, weapons, boxes of demolitions, flamethrowers, reels of telephone wire, and personal equipment from socks to toilet articles. Hundreds of brown lifebelts were washing to and fro, writhing and twisting like brown sea slugs. The waves broke around the disabled tanks, bulldozers and beached landing craft ... There was a wide stretch of sand being narrowed by the minute by the tide, then a sharply rising shingle bank of small, smooth stones that ended at the sea wall. Against the wall were soldiers of the first assault team. Some were scooping out shelters; a number were stretched out in the loose attitude of the wounded; others had the ultimate stillness of death; but most were just sitting with their backs against the wall.'
Lt Charles Cawthon, 2nd Bn, 116th Inf Regt, US 29th Inf Div (11)

'The .50 calibre and the .30 calibre machine-guns were left on the boat along with the bazookas and flamethrowers, there wasn't any question of getting them ashore — although they had been packed as floatable with extra life-jackets and large waterproof bags — we called them elephant's condoms. You could put a whole gun in them and tie the end up and keep it secure both from the water and the sand. Most of the chaps just got ashore with their pistol and cartridge belt and canteen and their rifle and perhaps their gas mask, which was a helluva good piece of equipment to keep your head up.'
Lt George Itzen, US 147th Engineer Combat Bn (12)

'Our only chance was to get off the beach as quick as possible because we were sitting ducks. While resting behind the obstacles, Private Gillingham, a young soldier, fell in beside me, white with fear ... His look was that of a child asking what to do. I said, "Gillingham, let's get separated as much as we can 'cause the Germans will fire at two quicker than one." ...
(cont. overleaf)

'I heard a shell coming and dove into the sand, face down. Shrapnel rose over my head and hit all around me, blowing me three or four feet. My rifle was ripped from my hand and my helmet went twenty-five or thirty feet in front of me. When I started to jump up and run, a sharp pain hit my spine from my neck to my lower back. I pulled myself by my elbows to my rifle ... and dragged myself into the hole the shell had made ...

'The shell that injured me took Gillingham's chin off, including the bone, except for a small piece of flesh. He tried to hold his chin in place as he ran ... He made it to the sea wall where Bill Hawkes and I gave him his morphine shot. We stayed with him for approximately thirty minutes until he died. The entire time, he remained conscious and aware that he was dying. He groaned in pain but was unable to speak.'

Pfc Warner Hamlett, 2nd Bn, 116th Inf Regt, US 29th Inf Div (13)

'Just before the landing all of our ... standard web gear, issue gear, fine battle-proven gear, was taken away from us because some theorist figured that it would be far easier and much more practical to wear a hunting-type jacket. So at the last minute we were issued with these canvas jackets with fantastic pockets all over the place and we transferred all our gear into these pockets.

'When we hit the bottom we had approximately four hundred yards to struggle through the water to the beach. There was small arms fire all around so you were up and down, ducking down ... Every time I got up I thought it was pure terror that was making my knees buckle until I finally hit the beach and realized I had about one hundred pounds of sand in the pockets of my jacket ... on top of the fifty or sixty-pound load we were all carrying in.

'When I finally got up the shale I had my first sergeant with me and I asked him, "For God's sake get a packet of cigarettes out", and he had to dig out handfuls of sand before he could get a pack out for me ...'

Capt Edward Wozenski, 2nd Bn, 16th Inf Regt, US 1st Inf Div (14)

'There was a hard jar to the side of my face, and blood started streaming off my chin. I don't recall any particular emotion on being hit for the first time, but I did realize that this was no place to linger; those along the embankment seemed much safer ... Having decided that survival, never mind valour, lay forward, I tried to rise but seemed to be hoisting the English Channel with me. The assault jacket's pockets, the gas-mask case, boots, leggings and uniform all held gallons of salt water

(Tim Hawkins)

... I now jettisoned the assault jacket and lumbered up the beach ... I took my .45 service automatic from its plastic bag and found it sticky with salt and gritty with sand. When I pulled the slide back to load a round into the chamber, it stuck halfway. The embankment was strewn with rifles, Browning automatics and light machine guns, all similarly fouled ...

'I left some of the able-bodied trying to clean weapons and ran down to the water-line ... From here the face of the bluffs and the exit road were visible and I expected to see flashes and smoke from German guns. The only smoke ... however, was from brush fires started by the naval cannonade. Under their smoke a few brave souls were climbing the bluff.'

Lt Charles Cawthon, 2nd Bn, 116th Inf Regt, US 29th Inf Div (15)

'As we approached the beach the ramp was lowered. Mortar and artillery shells exploded on land and in the water. Unseen snipers concealed in the cliffs were shooting down at individuals, but most havoc was from automatic weapons. The water was turning red from the blood ... There were dead men floating in the water and there were live men acting dead, letting the tide take them in. I was crouched down to chin-deep in the water when mortar shells began falling at the water's edge. Sand began to kick up from small-arms fire from the bluffs ... While lying half in and half out of the water, behind one of the log poles, I noticed a GI running from right to left ... An enemy gunner shot him as he stumbled for cover. He screamed for a medic. One of the aid men moved quickly to help him, and he also was shot. I will never forget

seeing that medic lying next to the wounded GI and both of them screaming. They died in minutes.'

Sgt Robert J. Slaughter, 1st Bn, 116th Inf Regt, US 29th Inf Div (16)

'Captain Zappacosta was the first man off and he was hit immediately. Machine-gun bullets were rattling off the boat. The next two men off were both hit and fell into the water, and I was the fourth man off. What saved my life was that the boat reared up and I went off the side of the ramp with a 30/40lb radio on my back, and went up to my neck in the water. I knew I couldn't keep the radio. Captain Zappacosta came up and mumbled something — I think he said, "Help me!" and he went back down and we never saw him again. I tried to get in closer and kept looking back at the craft and who was following, and they were being cut down just like you wouldn't believe. No one I have ever met until this day ... survived that boat. It was the command boat, with Captain Zappacosta on there, an officer from C Company was on there, the Forward Observer for the artillery was on there, some of the radio operators were on there ... it was the Headquarters boat for B Company'.

Sgt Robert L. Sales, 1st Bn, 116th Inf Regt, US 29th Inf Div (17)

'We were about 300 feet off the beach when our LST got hit ... so we had to swim in ... your only concern at that time was to reach your goal of the beach and the only way to do it was to get rid of the equipment. We had brought flamethrowers and machine guns ... which were vital to our

On top of the cliffs and bluffs behind Omaha were eight concrete bunkers and four open positions mounting guns of between 75mm and 88mm calibre, zeroed in to cover the whole length of the beach. These coastal batteries were targeted for bombing by 480 USAAF B-24 Liberators, followed up by heavy naval gunfire, craters from this bombardment were also supposed to provide plentiful cover for the infantry when they hit the beach. In the event none of the German gun emplacements was knocked out by the bombardment, and the beach was uncratered. (US National Archives)

attack but we had to let them go because the weight of them would have taken us under ... We were in about twelve feet of water and there were mines all around ... When I arrived on the beach, believe it or not, the only thing I had was myself. I had dropped my rifle in the water and when I hit the beach I laid there and thought to myself, "What am I going to do here? Am I going to wrassle, or fist fight, or what?" But other boys ... had been shot and were lay-ing near me and I took their rifles and belts ...

'Along the beach I had a buddy who was struck through the throat by a bullet and I was trying to press the reins to stop the bleeding, trying to hold it in. I ... was doing the best I could but he died in about two or three minutes.

'We finally made it to the bottom of the cliffs where we had more safety because the Germans could not fire their machine guns straight down ... Let me say that in our original company of 213 men, eight hours after we landed only thirty-eight were still in action.'

Pfc Robert Koch, 1st Bn, 116th Inf Regt, US 29th Inf Div (18)

(Tim Hawkins)

'I saw one of my sergeants ... his left thumb was gone but he didn't look as if he was hurt too badly so I called his name and told him to get up and come with us, and I rolled him over and he was dead, and just in front of him was another fellow ... lying there so I hollered at him "Let's get up and go"... and he kinda looked back over his shoulder at me and didn't say anything and when I got closer I saw that there was blood all over his back and he'd been hit in the stomach and the bullet had passed right through and come out of his spine, and so I started toward the sea wall ... and then I was hit by machine-gun fire in the left leg and the pain was terrible ... I managed to get up and then a sniper got me in my right leg ... I started out to cross the beach with thirty-five men and only six got to the top, that's all ... Bodies were spread everywhere, you could hardly walk on the sand for bodies ...'

Lt Robert Edlin, US 2nd Ranger Bn (19)

'I got a bullet through the top of my helmet and then, as I waded through deep water, carrying an M1 rifle at port arms, a bullet hit the receiver plate. I was able to fire the gun one time, then the stock broke in half ... Bullets ripped through my field jacket and one glanced off my helmet ... I noticed three amphibious tanks and two of them were knocked out. Many Company A soldiers were hanging on to the tanks, one of which was firing its 75mm into the pillbox on the right flank of Dog Green. The bunker just kept firing back.

'...A little in front of me, Private Robert Dittmar was hit in the chest. I heard him yell, "I'm hit, I'm hit" and watched him as he continued to go forward about ten more yards. He tripped over a tank obstacle ... He seemed to be suffering from shock and was yelling, "Mother, mother..." as he rolled around on the sand.

'Sergeant Barnes got shot down right in front of me and Lieutenant Donaldson. Sergeant "Pilgrim" Robertson had a gaping wound in ... his forehead. He was walking crazily in the water ... Then I saw him get down on his knees and start praying with his rosary beads.'

Pte Hal Baumgarten, 1st Bn, 116th Inf Regt, US 29th Inf Div (20)

'There was a 1st Division sergeant, who had seen combat in North Africa, and he said, "See that bunker next to the exit, get some fire on that baby." ... He sure knew what he was doing. We got up there and started firing on that embrasure. The sarge took some men with a bangalore torpedo and placed it ... He stopped that thing from murdering us ... It was a killer, and the man with the Big Red One on his shoulder helped us to blow it up.'

S/Sgt William H.Lewis, 1st Bn, 116th Inf Regt, US 29th Inf Div (21)

'Some of the assault units were issued with a 'special canvas assault jacket with large pockets front and back in which there were grenades, rations, mess gear, raincoat, a syrette of morphine, toilet articles, motion sickness pills, water purification tablets, DDT dusting powder, a paste to put on his boots in case [the soldier] encountered chemically contaminated areas, a small block of TNT. Around his waist was strapped an ammunition and equipment belt from which swung an entrenching tool, another first aid packet and a canteen. From his neck hung a special assault gas mask and extra bandoliers of ammunition. In addition, each man carried his individual weapon, and if a member of a machine-gun, mortar, flamethrower or demolition team, his part of that load ...' (Lt Charles Cawthon, 2nd Bn, 116th Inf Regt, US 29th Inf Div) (30)

'We both agreed we would have to get off the beach. George said, "Look, I'm a good swimmer and you're not badly hurt, let me swim you out to that knocked-out tank in the water out there."

'... We got out to the tank, which was in about three or four feet of water ... and hung onto the port side. At the rear there were three heads bobbing in the water. They were three men from the tank crew with their faces all powder burned. The tank commander, a buck sergeant, was sitting behind the turret with his left leg off at the knee and the bone and the artery floating in the water. He said that his men were of no value to him, they wouldn't do what he said and he was very upset with them. He asked us to get him a shot of morphine. Although my ankle was numb, I felt so happy to be on a firm surface that I crawled inside the turret, grabbed the first-aid pack and gave him a shot.'

Cpl Gilbert G. Murdoch, 1st Bn, 116th Inf Regt, US 29th Inf Div (22)

'When I crawled up the beach to the sea wall I had an M1 rifle, two bandoliers of ammo and several grenades. No helmet, no gas mask, no pack, because I had peeled them all off so I could swim. I crawled around to find a helmet from a dead buddy only to find it half full of head — I quickly found another. We were lying behind the sea wall re-grouping when General Cota walked up and said to Colonel Schneider, "I'm expecting the Rangers to lead the way." We started inland through a smoke haze and a field of Bouncing Betties and captured some Germans ... We proceeded up the Vierville Draw and drew fire from both sides and sniper fire from the church steeple. Colonel Schneider called for a naval bombardment of the church and it was promptly demolished. A girl sniper was found in the rubble.'

Sgt Victor H. Fast, US 5th Ranger Bn (23)

'There were dead people everywhere, there were people floating in the water, there were wrecked tanks, there were wrecked jeeps, there were tanks that were supposed to be floating in the water that were dead on land, and some of them had been knocked out by the 88[mm] guns which were firing straight down the beach ... We'd been told it would be a walk-over, we'd just walk on to the beach and the Germans would have been obliterated, the air force and the guns and the combat engineers, they'd make it so that the infantry could just walk ashore ... but it wasn't like that. Not at all.'

Lt Col Edwin Woolf, 6th Engineer Special Bde (24)

(Tim Hawkins)

The beach was swept from both flanks and at some points from straight ahead by direct fire from artillery and machine gun positions; it was pounded by indirect fire from mortars and artillery from the top of the bluffs; and above the high-water line it was sown with mines. Beyond the seawall heavy wire entanglements and concrete obstacles blocked the four 'draws' (gullies) which offered the only way off the beach. (US National Archives)

One of about 2,200 casualties suffered on Omaha Beach on D-Day, left by the retreating tide lying forlornly at the foot of a beach obstacle, his hasty first memorial a pair of crossed rifles.

The obstacles began about 150 yards below high-water mark, with ten-foot iron frames fitted with Teller mines or artillery shells. These tripods of heavy logs, some also mounting mines, were about 50 yards further in. Further in still were the steel rail 'hedgehogs' seen here in the left background; collision with these at any speed tore open the bottom of the flimsy landing craft. (US National Archives)

'The only thing I wanted was a cigarette and I asked this medic that was running across, "You got a dry cigarette?" and he handed me a cigarette and he was hit with something, I don't know what it was, but his entire body, his insides and everything, was blown all over me. It must have been a mortar that hit him ...'

Lt William H. Jones, US
467th AA Arty Bn (27)

'In all this fire, when you could hardly get across the beach and expect to live, Corporal Jones, a puny kid who was the last one to expect anything spectacular of, went out six times and brought men in. He checked one man over and could not move him. He came back to me, described the wound and asked me what he should do. He went back and did what he could. The man was shot through the chest. Jones could not drag him up, but he dragged in four men and survived. He should have got the DSC. Jones put on the best show that I saw on that beach.'

Capt C. N. Hall, medical officer,
2nd Bn, 16th Inf Regt,
US 1st Inf Div (25)

'After a couple of hours the tide started to come in and it washed many of our wounded buddies and some that were dead back into the Channel ... After being on the beach awhile, one of our tanks came ashore. I ran towards it to take cover and two of my buddies had the same idea. After a short time the Germans started to shoot at the tank. So I said to myself, "Get the hell away from this tank or you'll get killed." So I ran back to the same spot where I was before. I reached in my gas mask for some cigarettes and saw it was full of bullet holes. As I looked back at the tank I saw it backing up to take cover in the water. As it did so, it ran over my two buddies and killed them right there.'

Sgt Joe Pilck, 2nd Bn, 16th Inf Regt,
US 1st Inf Div (26)

'There was little or no firing from our troops. On the other hand, German machine guns, mortars and artillery pieces were laying down some of the heaviest fire I had ever experienced ... Somehow, [we] were able to get our half of the battalion headquarters across the soft sand and into the defilade afforded by the shingle embankment. I don't recall any casualties. Then, seeing some movement off the beach to our east, we began to move in that direction. En route we ran into Brigadier General Willard Wyman, our assistant divisional commander ... when General Wyman asked whether we were advancing by fire and movement, I answered, "Yes, sir. They're firing and we're moving."

Capt Albert H. Smith, 1st Bn,
16th Inf Regt, US 1st Inf Div (28)

(US National Archives)

'I remember floundering in the water ... trying to get my balance, when I was first shot through the palm of my left hand. I remember feeling nothing but a little sting at the time ... I made my way forward as best I could, but I was hit several other times, once in the left thigh, which broke a hip bone, although I didn't know it at the time. I remember being hit in the back a couple of times and feeling a tug as the chin strap of my helmet was severed by a bullet ... I staggered up against a wall and sort of collapsed there.

'I spent the whole day in the same position. Eventually the bodies of the other guys washed ashore and I was the only live one among so many of my friends, all of whom were dead and in many cases severely blown to pieces. It was not a very pleasant way to spend a day ... I guess about dusk, a couple of litter bearers came down and moved me.'

Sgt Thomas Valance, 1st Bn, 116th Inf Regt, US 29th Inf Div (29)

Despite the terrible losses suffered by the assault waves in the morning, by nightfall on 6 June some 40,000 men had come ashore over Omaha Beach. (US National Archives)

'Together we had been through months and years of wartime confusion and strains; marched countless tedious miles; lived in mud and dust, heat and cold. I knew their problems ... and they knew mine ... then it all came down to this brief first day of battle on the coast of Normandy, and, for so many of them, it all ended.'

Lt Charles Cawthon, 2nd Bn, 116th Inf Regt, US 29th Inf Div (30)

The British & Canadian Beaches

The British/Canadian invasion coast stretched about 24 miles, from Arromanches in the west to Ouistreham and the Orne river in the east.

The westernmost beach, Gold, reached from Asnelles west of Arromanches to La Rivière; it was assigned to the British 50th Inf Div, a veteran formation which had fought at El Alamein, in Sicily and Italy. Immediate tank support would be provided by 8th Armd Bde, and 47 Royal Marine Commando were to attack Port-en-Bessin on the right flank of Gold in order to link up with the Americans from Omaha. After seizing the beachhead the 50th Inf Div was to drive south to cut the Bayeux-Caen highway, and capture Bayeux.

Adjoining the left flank of Gold was Juno Beach, stretching five miles from La Rivière to St Aubin; this was assigned to the Canadian 3rd Inf Div and 2nd Armd Bde with support from 48 RM Cdo on their left flank. Followed up by elements of 51st Highland and 7th Armd Divs, their further mission was to strike south to the Bayeux-Caen highway and occupy Carpiquet airfield on the western edge of Caen.

The easternmost of all the beaches was Sword, separated from Juno by a gap of about three miles; Sword extended from Lion-sur-Mer in the west to Ouistreham in the east. Lion was the objective of 41 RM Cdo; the main assault formation was the British 3rd Inf Div, supported by the tanks of 27th Armd Bde, and on its extreme left flank by the Commandos of 1st Special Service Brigade. The Commandos' mission, after clearing the fortified buildings of Ouistreham, was to march inland to link up with the 6th Airborne troopers on the Orne bridges and the high ground beyond the river. The 3rd Inf Div was to drive south and capture Caen itself.

While many individuals among assault units had seen action before, particularly among the Commandos and some of the tank regiments, neither the 3rd British nor 3rd Canadian Inf Divs had combat experience as formations.

Apart from preliminary air and naval bombardment and the support of DD tanks, the British/Canadian beach forces had another asset denied the Americans: detachments from 79th Armd Div equipped with 'funnies' — specially modified tanks of a number of types, designed to clear paths through the defences. These included Sherman 'flails', which beat the ground ahead with chains and set off mines; 'bobbins', which laid rolls of artificial trackway across shingle for following tanks; 'crocodiles', which mounted large flamethrowers instead of guns; and AVREs — Armoured Vehicles Royal Engineers — which fired massive demolition mortars.

On Gold Beach the higher than expected tide and rough sea prevented both much of the planned clearance of obstacles, and the offshore launch of DD tanks. Luckily the 'funnies' made up to some extent for the lack of gun tank support, enabling the assault infantry to get across the beach, though at some cost and under continuing fire. On the left the West Country battalions of 231 Bde had very hard fighting in the fortified villages behind the beach, which lasted all afternoon; on the right 69 Bde got inland behind Arromanches with less difficulty and lower casualties.

At Juno the Canadians faced difficult conditions. Offshore rocks led the planners to delay landing to allow the tide to come in further, and this again hampered the obstacle clearing parties, who had little time to work and were under fire from 100 yards' range. The strongly fortified seafront at Courseulles and Bernières was defended by formidable gun emplacements and determined infantry. Many landing craft fouled the obstacles in rough water and were blown up, but the Canadians stormed ashore. On the crowded beach they took heavy losses to mines and crossfire without the support of the delayed DD tanks, but their grim determination to avenge their losses at Dieppe in 1942 carried them over the beach and seven miles inland.

On Sword Beach the fast tide, submerged obstacles, and failure to 'swim' the DD tanks ashore duplicated many of the problems at Juno; but here, too, just enough of the specialised armoured vehicles and gun tanks got into action to support the infantry across the beach. The built-up area of Ouistreham and Riva Bella behind the beach had been strongly fortified and garrisoned — the latter had 22 artillery pieces including 12 massive 155 mm guns — and vicious house-to-house fighting lasted until midday. The Commandos of 1st Special Service Bde

(Martin Brayley)

managed to link up with the Airborne troops as planned, and 3rd Inf Div got some six miles inland by nightfall. The 3rd Bn, King's Shropshire Light Infantry with a squadron of Shermans from the Staffordshire Yeomanry actually got within two miles of Caen that evening before being forced back for lack of support.

A dangerous four-mile salient between the British on Sword and the Canadians on Juno was still held by the Germans, but without armour they could not exploit it. The 21st Pz Div, based near Caen, started moving toward the British beaches early on the morning of 6 June, but the chaotic German chain of command produced confused orders and counter-orders which stopped them intervening until it was too late. Mechanised infantry - Panzer-Grenadiers - of this crack division advanced into the salient and reached the coast by 2000 hours; but their tank support was stopped dead by Canadian and British artillery and RAF air attack.

Infantry disembark from a Landing Craft Assault (LCA), the British version of the American LCVP; in the background are two Landing Craft Tank (LCTs). The shoebox-like LCA/LCVP 'Higgins boats' relied on the power of their screws and the rising tide to get off the beach after landing their loads. All the heavier landing craft and landing ships dropped stern anchors while some way off the beach; after running in and unloading they winched themselves off again by means of the anchor chains. (IWM B5245)

GOLD

'As we closed in to the shore ... the fighter-bombers started to come over, and the Royal Navy opened up from behind ... There were terrific explosions from the shore which was soon a large haze of smoke and small fires ... The landing craft bearing the flails [mine-clearing tanks] came past us ... to make gaps in the beach mines for the infantry and ourselves ...

'We were now about 700 yards from the shore and as the ramp was lowered I could see two of the flails brewing up just to my front ... The very intricate operation of launching my tank from the craft into the very unpleasantly choppy sea soon drove away any further speculation ... Without more ado I gave my driver the order to go and down the ramp we went. The screen was very flimsy in the rough sea and water poured in everywhere ... when I saw that things were hopeless, I gave the order to bale out. I can only imagine that the first shell which landed was our undoing ... it must have holed one of the bottom plates.

'Corporal Footitt pressed the button on our rubber dinghy which inflated automatically ... I scrambled inside the turret to get my map-case out, but we were going down so fast I had no time ... A few seconds later our tank ... disappeared into the murky depths ... We managed to hail an LCG which came over to pick us up, and we were bracketed by high-explosive as we climbed on board ... The Navy, as always, treated us magnificently, and we breakfasted on whisky and Mars bars ...'

Lt Stuart Mills, DD tank commander, Sherwood Rangers Yeomanry, British 8th Armd Bde (1)

'We prepared to land at 0650 on 6th June on Jig Green beach near Le Hamel. As the driver, I took the Churchill AVRE down the ramp into the sea. Most of us were suffering from sea sickness. We bottomed in about six feet of water, which meant ... my periscope was blocked by the sea water. I seemed to drive for hours totally blind, although it was only a few seconds. Suddenly my periscope began to clear and I could see a sandy beach dotted with gun emplacements and tank traps. The roar of engines and the sound of exploding shells seemed insignificant now that we were on dry land. There was a babble of shouts from the crew, my seasickness disappeared. We had arrived.'

Spr R .J. Mellen, British 82nd Assault Sqn, Royal Engineers (2)

'The memories are still with all who took part. Memories of underwater marines in skin suits [frogmen] floating dead in the sea ... of soldiers with the African Ribbon on their chests lying dead on the beach.'

Dvr E. G. Sergeant, British 73rd Field Co, Royal Engineers (3)

'I saw the ... beach quite clearly, black-looking tanks crawled along it like squat stag beetles. One tank was ... burning with a hot transparent red flame ... There came a terrible, roaring explosion and I felt the shock of it through my boots. A great pillar of smoke and debris shot high into the air on our starboard bow until it became a great, spreading tree over a hundred feet high ... That must have been one of our LCAs, it was only fifty yards away.

'I stepped down from the bow ... into only a couple of inches of water ... By the third step I was onto dry land and running, bangalore torpedo in my left hand and rifle in my right, after the rest of the troop. Everyone seemed to be heading ... towards the shelter of the sea wall, the machine gun was still firing long bursts though no one seemed to be hit ... My way lay close to a burning tank ... I felt the heat of the flames on my face and made a wide detour ... A khaki-clad figure lay almost across my path, curled up on his left side ... His knees were drawn up and his arms folded across his chest. His head was bent forward so that his face was turned towards me but where his face should have been was a featureless, red mask.'

Marine Frank Wright, British 47 RM Cdo (4)

'The AVREs on the beach all seemed to have been knocked out. We did not find the gaps we expected. The beach was raked with enfiladed fire, and there was an anti-tank gun in a concrete and steel emplacement in Le Hamel. The Germans did not show much sign of giving up. I realized we would have to gap our way through ourselves, using bangalores which we had with us. Casualties began to pile up. While gapping our way off the beach, I saw the OC limping badly. He had been hit by mortar fragments as he left his LCA. He told me to take command of the Battalion. A Company who should have landed close to Le Hamel, climbed the sea wall, and silenced the opposition, had almost ceased to exist ... '

Maj Warren, 1st Bn, Hampshire Regt, British 50th Inf Div (5)

In the lee of a disabled Churchill **AVRE** tank of one of the Royal Engineer Assault Squadrons, and amidst the dead of the first wave ashore, medics treat British casualties. The AVRE was fitted with a 290mm muzzle-loading mortar or 'petard', which fired a massive 40lb bomb over short ranges but with devastating effects on enemy gun emplacements. Churchills were used as the basis of several types of 'funnies' deployed by 79th Armoured Division units on D-Day, especially fascine and bridging tanks to fill or cross ditch obstacles. Despite heavy losses these — like the Sherman 'flails' which cleared paths through the minefields — played an important part in getting British and Canadian infantry quickly inland off the beaches. (IWM B5095)

(Martin Brayley)

'There was quite a shambles on the beach. The flail tanks which were supposed to clear the main exit lane through the minefield had been knocked out. Fortunately, an extremely brave Sapper officer offered to clear a secondary lane manually. We gave him and his small party covering fire. Of the squadron's nineteen original tanks, only five were still mobile and I ordered [them] down the lane. We were engaged by an anti-tank gun firing from a concrete casemate. He scored a direct hit on the leading tank, destroying the gun mantlet ... With all five guns ... we managed to silence him. We then turned on to the road leading to Le Hamel ... we were overtaken by one of the AVRE Churchill tanks ... The sergeant in command said that he was the sole survivor of his troop ... It appeared that the main enemy fire was coming from a large ... many-storied house. I ordered the Churchill [AVRE] forward to demolish the house with the petard ... Maximum covering fire was given by the Sherman tanks ... The petard fired and something like a small flying dustbin hit the house just above the front door. It collapsed like a pack of cards, spilling the defenders with their machine guns, anti-tank weapons and an avalanche of bricks into the courtyard.'

Maj Peter Selerie, Sherwood Rangers Yeomanry, British 8th Armd Bde (8)

'Not much organization on the beach ... dotted everywhere were sodden bundles — men of the Hampshires, Devons and Dorsets that had led the infantry spearhead. Tanks still burning, LCTs blown up by mines, houses afire, craters, smells, Achtung Minen and skulls and crossbones. Mine casualties ... were very common and some were most frightful to see. My most vivid recollection was being called suddenly to see a man ... lying on a door in the back of a truck. All was covered with a blanket save for his head. He had no face that was not raw and torn, and his eyes were dull and opaque, wrinkled like those of a dead fish. He was conscious and moaning. I put my hand under the blanket and felt for his wrist. To my horror all I could find was a bloody stump — and it was the same on the other side. He had a gash in his stomach, and a large wound in his thigh ... I gave him a large dose of morphia, bound up his stumps and sent him to the ASC. Later I heard that he was "doing well".'

Dr Peter Johnson, British Royal Army Medical Corps (6)

'Before me was about forty yards of heaving sea reaching almost up to my chest, and ahead a slowly-rising beach covered with round, flat stones ... Away to my left other landing craft were disgorging their loads, a tank was blazing and exploding ... It seemed an age before I reached the shore ... All at once a tank close to my left blew up, and scattered fragments of jagged metal flew over my head. Meanwhile, shells from our warships still screamed over our heads, together with bullets from our own craft just out to sea...

'[A] large bomb crater ... was already filling up with German troops who had been taken prisoners, and one or two of them proved to have been wounded. They all looked dazed and shaken. One was Polish, another Russian, while another, who had a Red Cross painted on his helmet, told me he came from Dortmund.'

Pte R. S. McDowall, 5th Bn, East Yorkshire Regt, British 50th Inf Div (7)

British infantry take cover after landing. The very dense beach obstacles and an unusually high tide seriously hampered the assault waves; but the bombardment was effective against many of the German defensive emplacements, which were mostly built into houses in the straggling villages along the seafront immediately behind the level beaches. These were strongly defended, however, and the last of them were taken only after bitter and costly street fighting. (IWM B5090)

'Scanning the beaches with field glasses, I was astonished to observe the exact resemblance of the scene before me to the model we had made, in spite of the devastation wrought in the area by sustained bombings and naval guns, the conspicuous landmarks were undamaged. I saw too an occasional flash presumably from the 88mm (spotted in the aerial photograph), now used as an anti-tank gun. The most horrific sight I witnessed was the action of one of our flamethrower [tanks] attacking a troublesome force occupying a small chateau adjacent to the beach. A couple of bursts from that fiery dragon sent the dwelling up in rolling volumes of smoke and flame. A few seconds later I could see through the gaps which were once windows a raging furnace within.'

V. J. Galliano, No 9 Beach Group, British 21st Army Group HQ (9)

'My three platoon commanders were dead and all the platoon sergeants were wounded ... The brigadier came and said the Hampshires' name was at the top of the list for doing so well. I had expected a blast for taking twelve hours for a four-hour task ...

'I went back with Colour Sergeant Eastburn in the carrier and it was midnight when my day's work was done. We issued blankets and I had a bit of chocolate and a biscuit and a drink of water before turning in for two hours' sleep ... Casualties had been heavy. A Company were left with Tony Boyd, their second-in-command, and 27 men, B and C about 55 each. D Company only lost about 25. A high proportion of officers were killed or wounded. I think some 270 casualties out of 700 were sustained on D-Day.'

Capt A. R. C. Mott, 1st Bn, Hampshire Regt, British 50th Inf Div (10)

'If a German soldier appeared, everybody fired at him. It was no bother, we didn't think of them as human beings ... You are there, there is noise, everybody is shouting and screaming and suddenly you see this figure. In the excitement you fire at him ... Without bragging about being a good shot, a man only 100 or 150 yards away is an awful big target ... Some Germans were trying to surrender but in the excitement we fired on them before they had any chance ... I don't think our lads

were saying, well, I don't care if that man wants to surrender ... I don't think that was in anyone's mind. I think it was the excitement of constantly stuffing fresh ammunition into magazines and blazing away. A lot of men were just firing from the hip as we walked forward, not taking their rifles up to the shoulder and taking individual aim ... There was a lot of small arms fire, more than you would think ...

'We started digging in for the night at about nine o'clock, just as it was coming dusk ... I never stopped to eat all day; I hadn't even taken the cork out of my water bottle. I had grabbed water from water butts and out of streams ... I never closed my eyes all night, I was far too excited. I did get a sense of relief that I'd got through the day ... we were awful thin on the ground: ten of us set off that morning but only four or five of us were still there that night ...'

Pte Dennis Bowen, 5th Bn,
East Yorkshire Regt,
British 50th Inf Div (11)

(Martin Brayley)

No 6 Commando from Lord Lovat's 1st Special Service Bde landing on Sword Beach wearing their green berets rather than steel helmets. The brigade fulfilled their dual mission: to push inland as fast as possible to link up with the 6th Airborne troops holding the Orne river and Caen canal bridges, and to clear Ouistreham in heavy house-to-house fighting. (IWM B5103)

JUNO

'We were right in close now and the Bren on our craft opened fire straight ahead and we weaved in and out between the ugly tripods standing in the water, with big black bottles full of explosive on the end ... The last thing I saw before I ducked my head was one of the craft about a hundred yards to our left blown sky-high from a direct hit ... A few seconds later we felt the scrape as the craft struck the sandy beach, and in no time the door was down and we were leaping into the foam.'

Pte Don Doner, Queen's Own Rifles of Canada, Canadian 3rd Inf Div (12)

'Our Support Craft was knocked out so we had no heavy weapons. The DD tanks had not come ashore. My platoon, approximately 36 strong, went through what we believe was enfilade fire from five machine-guns. The official battalion killed in action figures on 6 June 1944 numbered 63, B Company, 34. I don't have the figures for the platoon but I do know that only nine men moved inland, three of whom were walking wounded. Of the ten men in my section, seven were killed and two wounded. Of these ten men, six had been in the unit since June 1940. The one survivor, the latest replacement, had never done a "landing" in training.'

L/Cpl Rolph Jackson, Queen's Own Rifles of Canada, Canadian 3rd Inf Div (13)

'I didn't realise we were under fire until I saw two men collapse and fall over the starboard side. By then it was too late to beat a retreat, and I later found three bullet holes in my map case ... they must have passed between my arm and body during that period ...

'The beach was covered with casualties, some Canadian, some British. The surf was incredible, with beached and half-sunken craft wallowing about in it ... Some tanks struggled ashore and some bogged in the shingle. Those ... advancing had their turret lids shut and were heading for a large group of wounded. I was sickened to see one run over two of our wounded, and ... heading for our good padre, John Armstrong, who had been badly wounded in the thigh ... I ran back down the beach and hammered on the turret, to try to get someone to put his head out. When this failed I stuck a Hawkins anti-tank grenade in the sprocket and blew the track off — that stopped it.'

Capt Dan Flunder, British 48 RM Cdo (14)

'Mortar and artillery fire saturated the beach area, a burst of machine-gun fire swathed through our small group, leaving six or more men killed or wounded. We reached the limited shelter of the sand dunes and established a command post ... A formidable concrete German command post dominated our beach ... [and] grenades were hurled through the gun ports. Germans emerged with their hands up ... Germans appeared from everywhere, surrendering in droves, but we were still harassed by mortar fire from beyond the beach.'

Maj Max Morrison, 8th Bn, King's (Liverpool) Regt (15)

(Right) One of the four casemates of the Merville battery today; and the view west towards Sword Beach. On the night of 5/6 June 1944 the battery's 75mm guns were targeted for destruction by 750 men of Lt Col Otway's 9th Parachute Bn, inserted partly by air drop nearby and partly by gliders crash-landing inside the battery's strong ground defences. A scattered drop and missing equipment forced Otway to attack the battery with about 150 lightly-armed men — considerably fewer than the German garrison. The paratroopers took the objective, at a cost of some 50 per cent casualties. (Will Fowler)

(Martin Brayley)

'We reached shore safely and raced over the beach to the dunes. Sand had piled up against the sea wall, making it easily passable, but it was soon apparent that the pill-box on our right housed an 88mm gun which was firing on the landing craft and causing extreme damage. We were now coming under heavy fire from inland. ... By this time I had been wounded twice, once by a mortar and once by a shell fragment which pierced my arm, rendering it useless ... I then went to a tank which had its turret closed, and tried banging on the armament with my Sten gun, without success, and it was at this time that, probably in shock and weakened by loss of blood, I collapsed to the ground.

'After the beach had been cleared, the remnant of my platoon, consisting of a sergeant and ten men, passed by, taking the maps from my pack and pressing on to join the company.'

Lt Peter Rea, Queen's Own Rifles of Canada, Canadian 3rd Inf Div (16)

'Too many of us had bunched behind the sea wall and the second wave was now coming ashore. In order to get the men moving ... I stood in the open and shouted at the top of my voice ... Apparently a sniper ... was watching for just such an indication of authority and laid a sight in the middle of my back. At the instant he squeezed the trigger fate invited me to turn, facing the water, so that I met the bullet ... [it] passed through my arm, entered my chest under my armpit and ploughed on, coming out through the middle of my back. I didn't know that at the time because a mortar shell landed at the same instant and I spun around and fell flat on my face. Rising again, I discovered my left arm was useless. Someone pulled me down and I didn't stand again for a month.'

Lt G. V. Moran, North Shore (New Brunswick) Regt, Canadian 3rd Inf Div (17)

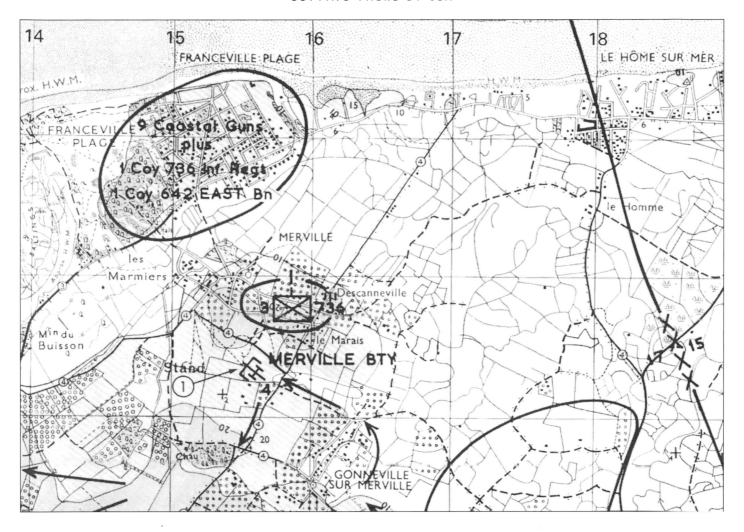

(Below) Symbolic of the successful link-up by British airborne and seaborne forces south-east of Sword Beach on 6 June: two of the most dangerous ways to go to war — a glider and a DD 'swimming' tank. The Sherman from 27th Armd Bde is still encumbered with the collapsed 'skirt' of metal tubing and canvas, though it has blown away its tall exhaust stack. Although the sea was too rough for safe launching at the distance from shore envisaged in the Allied plan, the DD concept did work, and those which did get ashore surprised the German defenders and gave valuable support to the assault infantry. Their other main failure lay in their slow water speed; intended to spearhead the landings, they were usually overtaken by the infantry landing craft on the way in. The majority were landed directly on the beaches, and these got into action first. (IWM B5348)

Immediately the beach exits had been cleared the follow-up landings of vehicles and equipment began, to get as many machines and as much matériel ashore before dark as was humanly possible; the Allied plans had to anticipate heavy counter-attacks, particularly from German armoured divisions, and the assault infantry needed as much support as they could get. These DUKWs — an amphibious version of an American 2½-ton truck — could be launched from davits or the ramps of LCTs, and could drive straight up the beach. Some were swamped when launched too far out during the initial assault, but they were invaluable during the build-up phase. (IWM B5154)

SWORD

'We grounded on the beach at H hour, the ramp was lowered and the AVRE tanks went off and up the beach under the close covering fire of our Oerlikon guns, then there was a loud explosion and a lot of black smoke from the flotilla leader's LCT on our starboard side caused by a German 88mm shell hitting the tank containing the colonel of Engineers who was killed instantly; the hatch of this tank was thrown open and the sergeant driver climbed out and ran around the deck screaming and holding his head.'

Lt John Godwin, Royal Marines (18)

'As we hit the beach, I went forrard to see if the bows had been shot over their rollers. The party of seamen — four or six — were a mass of duffel-coats, steel helmets, teeth, jaws, brains and blood. There was a sweet sickly smell, stronger than all the cordite, grease, and oil normally present in almost any small craft in action ... Wading to the water's edge, I could not help noticing the number of battle-dressed bodies, all face down, gently floating on the tide line surrounded by a pinkish tinge.'

Lt Alex Sudborough, 45 RM Cdo, British 1st Special Service Bde (19)

'Almost in, 400 yards to go when my AVRE had a violent shake, we had been hit. Damage not known, because the LCT had also sustained damage a bit forward and we had to get off at once.

'The LCT stopped; again my AVRE was hit. Going down the ramp now and the water was almost up to our cupola. Again we were hit ... Coming out of the water, hit again, and at last dry and following the Troop Leader's AVRE up the sand. Hit a mine, one bogie gone, out following the leading AVRE's track, we were ordered to put up a windsock [to mark the route]. Struck a second mine, two bogies gone and left track gone. Two of the crew jumped out to put up a windsock, one blown up by a mine as he came round the tank, take all arms, and jumped out myself, destroying slidex and code papers. We were all out now, petrol was pouring out of the AVRE and filling the mine crater.'

Sgt T. R. Kilvert, British 77th Assault Sqn, Royal Engineers (20)

Tank crews rest in a Norman field. By nightfall on 6 June some 25,000 men had come ashore over Gold Beach and 29,000 over Sword; British casualties were about 400 and 630 men respectively. Juno, the most bitterly defended of the eastern beaches, cost the Canadians 1,000 casualties, but nevertheless they had made the deepest penetrations inland by nightfall — some seven miles, reaching but failing to take Carpiquet airfield. (IWM 5033)

'I would be the first to wade ashore two minutes after AVRE tanks had landed and they would be available to assist us in removing beach obstacles .... We hit the beach and were met by withering machine gun fire; the sand was spurting up in front of us ... Together with my eight Sappers [I] knelt in the water under the cover of the partly submerged obstacles. Most of the [AVREs] were knocked out. I shouted to make for the two end tanks ... We ran for our lives for the safety of one of the tanks and even then the other tank got hit ...

'It was late afternoon and a rollcall was taken. We had suffered heavy casualties ... D Day and the days afterwards ... cost three officers and eighteen other ranks killed, two officers and forty-two other ranks wounded and four missing ... Many old faces were no longer seen in the leaguer area. The old 9th was dead.'

L/Cpl K. Hollis, British 62nd/9th Field Sqn, Royal Engineers (21)

'Trembling, my rifle tightly clutched, I crouched awaiting the dreaded shout of "Ramps down". We seemed to inch in, in between craft already beached, some of which were burning ... This was it — I was determined to present myself for a minimum of time as a target ... and being one of the first off I had a clear run. On the order to go, I leapt up, bounded down the ramp, jumped and landed in about four feet of cold sea-water. I... waded as quickly as I was able to the shallows and the beach. My impression of the scene there was a complete shambles. Had the whole thing failed, was it a gigantic cock-up? Against a backcloth of smoke [and] gutted blazing buildings were several burning knocked-out DD tanks and strewn about from the water's edge up to the sea wall were sodden khaki bundles staining red the sand where they lay ... But there was no time to be staring at my first experience of corpses, a mad dash up the beach to gain ... the shelter of the sea wall. Find some sort of hole. Keep your head well down and try to locate a beach exit.'

Pte Richard Harris, 1st Bn, Suffolk Regt, British 3rd Inf Div (22)

'The LCTs go full speed ahead and it is a race for the shore. We land at 0725 hours and the impact nearly shoots the tanks through the doors. The flails stream out in three feet of water, followed by the AVREs. We are met by shell, mortar and SS and 75 AP and small arms fire at 300 yards range ... Several tanks are hit as the landing craft doors go down ... [We] open fire on concrete gun emplacements, houses and dug-in infantry. Tanks are brewing up right and left ... [We] get within fifty yards of our gapping places and open fire right into the slots of gun emplacements ...One flail tank strikes a sunken obstacle with a mine on it and the bottom is blown in ... Lieutenant Allen has three 88mm AP straight through into the turret and all but one of the crew are killed ... An 88 AP goes straight into the front of Sergeant Cochran's ... The East Yorks and the South Lancs are now streaming up the beach covered by fire from the beach clearing flails ... Bridging AVREs dropped their bridges, but the crews jump out to make them fast and in doing so are killed or wounded and the tanks receive direct hits and are brewed up. German soldiers rush from the houses shouting and firing as they come and soon the beach is strewn with dead and wounded of our own and enemy troops.'

Capt Tim Wheway, 22nd Dragoons, British 79th Armd Div (23)

'We made good progress, the tank behaving magnificently in a sea which would have daunted many a larger craft ... We beached, but ... hit an anti-tank obstruction ... With our canvas already deflated, the sea just poured in, naturally stopping the engine ... Still, as our orders were to destroy any houses left standing in the village we just stayed put, and kept the gun firing. But soon the water was halfway up the inside of the turret, so we had no option but to "bale out"... Only three of us out of our crew of five were destined to reach the shore ... Our operator was never seen again ... The driver was picked up and taken back to England more dead than alive ...

'During the day I passed the survivors of tanks of the Staffordshire Yeomanry who had been blown up ... outside Hermanville. They passed like zombies with burnt uniforms and staring eyes, oblivious to their surroundings. At that time I had never seen anyone badly shocked before and their appearance and burnt hands and faces frightened me when I thought of the days ahead.'

Lt R. Cadogan, British 27th Armd Bde (24)

'I found a disorganised group of engineers crouching in a deserted pill-box and, as I passed to see if I could not break through the wire at that point, an enemy sniper put a bullet clean through the skull of a man lying at length, and, as he imagined, in safety on

Behind Sword Beach a Commando officer (left) confers with a counterpart from 3rd Inf Div flanked by signallers. In 1944 man-portable radios such as the standard British No 18 set used by infantry companies were much less reliable than today's equipment, and poor communication caused many deaths because of the difficulty of co-ordinating fire and movement. Valves in the sets would fail without warning; batteries were heavy, and had only a short life in constant use; and reception was always 'drifting' from the signal. The only truly reliable communication was by the old land-line field telephone, but the obvious practical difficulty ruled this out during most types of operations. (IWM B5065)

the sand. We began to run through the gap I had seen on the right. The men floundered in the loose sand under their top-heavy loads of ammunition and I ran up and down the line yelling them on with every curse I remembered ... Other troops, with the stupidity of sheep, were digging in along the length of the wire; they had not sense enough to realise that the enemy would blast it as conscientiously as a drill routine. One man sitting upright as if he was alone on the sands, clutched his knee and wept over the bloody mess.'

Lt Douglas Grant, British Royal Engineers (25)

Later I started crawling through the corn and came across a path cut through ... I did not think anything of it at the time, but doing it nearly finished my life. I crawled about six or seven yards and came across a body lying across the path. I crawled over it, and I think I passed over about six or seven. I had just crawled over the last one when this burst of machine-gun fire came over my head ... It must have been a German machine-gun on fixed lines at the other end of the passage.'

Pte C. J. Potter, 1st Bn, South Lancashire Regt, British 3rd Inf Div (26)

'Down we went into waist-deep sea about 30 yards from the water's edge. I can remember getting out of the water by a DD tank (Sherman) and pausing behind it. However, in the rather grey and overcast weather I noticed that sparks appeared on the turret caused, I imagine, by bullet strikes ...

'... Some of the local people came out into the street. I was handed a bottle by a middle-aged Frenchman and ... found it to be a strong rawish spirit which I later discovered was distilled cider (Calvados). We soon went through this village , and into open country until we came to the [Orne river and canal] bridges. I can remember the bullets striking the ironwork ... As I ran across one of the bridges I stopped near a dead British officer who had a Colt automatic .45 pistol attached to his neck with a lanyard. I broke the lanyard by putting my boots on it... and secured the pistol in an inner pocket of my BD blouse. This pistol came in very handy later on. This officer was one of the glider party that had landed during the night and did such good work capturing the bridges intact.'

Tpr P. H. B. Pritchard, No 6 Cdo, British 1st Special Service Bde (27)

'... With minimum delay, we pressed on in single file with 6 Commando in the lead. The whole brigade was in single file, so the more certainly to penetrate the coastal defences — 4 Commando detaching leftwards so as to take and clear all strongpoints in the town of Ouistreham. As we traversed the straight road approaching Hermanville we passed a small cluster of cottages ... At the doorway of one ... stood an old lady dressed wholly in black, gazing at us as we passed. She stood absolutely still and said no word but she was weeping all the time, making no attempt to hide or wipe away her tears. She was the only one to be seen, which wasn't at all surprising.'

Lt L. W. Bridger, HQ, British 1st Special Service Bde (28)

'Later on D-Day, 185 Brigade had reached the Benouville-Beuville area and I was with D Company, the forward company. When the gliders came in one of them slid across a field and hit two of our signallers who were operating a set in the ditch. They had their earphones on and didn't hear it coming ... one of them was decapitated.

'We dug in that night in a small village and I was lucky in that place. We just had a 24-hour pack ... bits of cheese and stuff. The first big trench I sat down in for the night was in somebody's back garden, with onions all around me, and I was able to eat my little bit of cheese with some spring onions.

'Although it seemed a long way from home, it was homely from the fact of being in a battalion like the Warwicks ... they were all local Birmingham lads, and in between the shells falling and the general noise of war, you could hear a heated argument going on about the merits of Villa and Birmingham City football clubs in a couple of slit trenches just behind you, and it seemed then as if you weren't so far from home.'

Pte Geoff Peters, 2nd Bn, Warwickshire Regt, British 3rd Inf Div (29)

Staying There
The Battle for the Bocage June-August 1944

By nightfall on 6 June a total of between 155,000 and 175,000 Allied troops had come ashore over the beaches or from the air. Total casualties in killed, wounded and missing of all services were about 6,500 Americans, 3,000 British and 1,000 Canadians — far fewer than had been anticipated. (All the above figures are estimates — sources vary considerably, and on the day conditions hardly allowed exact compilation of statistics.)

The invasion had been expected when high tide came at first light, in calm weather. It apparently did not occur to the German staff that a rising tide would allow landing craft to unload their troops and then float off again for another load; they also considered the weather on 6 June unacceptable for a landing. The consequent absence of many German senior officers from their posts and the failure of their subordinates to take decisive action had crippled any active defence. The static defences forming the Atlantic Wall had all been pierced in a matter of hours.

The only German armoured reserves held within reach, hampered as much by the Führer's indecision and a chaotic chain of command as by Allied air attacks, had failed to reach the battlefield. The Kriegsmarine had offered no resistance: the only Allied ship lost — a Norwegian destroyer — had been sunk by a mine. The Luftwaffe, whose potential threat to the masses of almost immobile shipping had haunted Allied planners, had virtually failed to appear. Cripplingly short of trained pilots and fuel, and overstretched once the Allied bombers returned to their strategic campaign over the Reich, the Luftwaffe would continue to offer no serious opposition. Allied air power had successfully cut off the invasion coast from the rest of France, and the arrival of German reinforcements would be piecemeal, over as long as two weeks. The beachheads would all link up by 12 June, and meanwhile rapid reinforcement and consolidation took place.

The initial objectives for all the landing forces had proved far too optimistic, however. On the British/Canadian front the capture of Caen, a vital objective for the first day, would in fact take more than a month of very costly fighting. In the west it would take the Americans until the end of June to clear the Cotentin Peninsula and capture Cherbourg. Meanwhile some of the Wehrmacht's finest divisions would be thrown into what became a three-month battle, stopping Allied advances dead and launching aggressive counter-attacks in a terrain which partly negated the Allies' advantages in numbers and air power.

This battle would be fought out in the terrible *bocage* country, a broken, wooded, claustrophobic landscape perfect for defensive fighting by small German units, and a nightmare for Allied commanders trying to co-ordinate advances. Names such as Hill 112, the Odon valley and St Lô would become grimly memorable in Allied divisional histories as the graveyards of thousands of men and hundreds of tanks.

On 25 July, while the bulk of the German armour was held around Caumont and Caen by Montgomery's armies, Gen Bradley launched the US 1st Army in Operation 'Cobra' southwards towards Coutances and Avranches, breaking out of southern Normandy. Gen Patton's newly arrived US 3rd Army swept first into Brittany, then south and east in a great hook towards the Seine. Gen Hodges' US 1st Army swung east and north towards Argentan, while Canadian, British and Polish divisions attacked southwards towards Falaise, forming a huge 'pocket' in which the bulk of the German 7th Army was trapped by 21 August. Allied artillery and aircraft caused carnage among the retreating enemy, and the Wehrmacht suffered some 60,000 casualties and a huge loss of matériel. In the last week of August the Allied armies swung north-east like a huge gate, crossing the Seine and entering Paris on 25 August.

On 7 June, D+1, men of the US 2nd Inf Div come ashore across Omaha Beach. New divisions were pouring in over all the invasion beaches while the prefabricated 'Mulberry harbours' were assembled and anchored off the US and British beachheads. By 9 June the 90th Inf Div would also be ashore; by 13 June, the 9th Inf and 2nd Armd Divs; by the end of June, the 30th and 79th Inf Divs, as well as scores of non-divisional armour, artillery and other support units. (US National Archives)

In the British sector the first follow-up divisions were the 7th Armd and 51st Highland Divs, veterans of years of combat in the North African desert and Italy, followed by the 49th and 43rd Inf Divs, and 11th and Guards Armd Divs:

'The Jock, as he prepared to go ashore, was a sadly burdened creature. First, as a basis, he wore boots, battle-dress, and a steel helmet. Next came his web equipment, to which were attached ammunition pouches, two waterbottles, a small and bulging haversack slung at the side, a bayonet, and an enormous pack round which a blanket had been bound with pieces of string. Next, on top of all that had gone before, were a respirator and a lifebelt. If he were lucky, he carried a rifle: if unlucky, a Bren gun, a two-inch mortar, or a load of two-inch mortar bombs done up in sacking and worn round his neck like a horse-collar. If any man had gone overboard he would have sunk like a brick, lifebelt and all.

'And to all this was added the invasion wader, a garment of repulsive design and doubtful utility, elephant-waisted and duck-footed, made of green oiled cotton, and (we found) extremely liable to split. As the seat was cut so as to admit the small haversack and the two waterbottles as well as other necessary portions of the wearer, the invasion wader must go down as the least becoming garment in history ... We struggled ashore through the fast-receding tide and dropped our waders and lifebelts on the beach ....'

(Capt Alastair Borthwick,
5th Bn, Seaforth Highlanders,
British 51st Highland Div —
Juno Beach, D+1) (1)

67

A violent Channel storm lasted from 19 to 22 June, badly damaging the British Mulberry harbour, wrecking the US one and seriously disrupting the build-up of supplies for the twenty Allied divisions now ashore. Some reinforcements for the beachhead were forced to ride out the storm on shipboard for four wretched days:

'On 19 June, after an incredibly turbulent Channel crossing, we were anxiously waiting to disembark on the tenuously held beachhead at Arromanches. The weather had taken a turn for the worse — which we had never thought possible ... the near gale-force winds made disembarkation an impossibility for the time being ... Deep in the lower decks and holds of the Ben Macree we were beginning to suffer the miseries of sea-sickness. Although at anchor, the ship tossed and rolled like a cork in the high winds and the enormous swell of the seas. The stink of hot oil from the nearby engine room proved disastrous to most stomachs and the toilet facilities, which may have been adequate under normal circumstances, were useless to cope with the sudden demand.'
(Cpl Douglas Proctor, 4th Bn, Somerset Light Infantry, British 43rd Inf Div (2) (Photo US National Archives)

(Martin Brayley)

Front Line Rations

'A compo box measured roughly two-and-a-half feet by one-and-a-half by one-and-a-half, and it contained a day's ration for fourteen men in a form which could easily be divided. Breakfast might be [soya link] sausages and beans; lunch, biscuits (the new thin kind), jam, butter, cheese, tea; dinner, meat-and-vegetables and a steamed pudding. Also in the box were a bar of chocolate, six boiled sweets, and seven cigarettes per man; and there were packets of salt and matches. There was even a ration of toilet paper. Everything was tinned and all the tins were small, so that they could be emptied at a sitting, and heating in water was all the cooking required.

'The food was of the very best quality: the puddings were rich and sweet, and the strawberry jam had strawberries in it. There were seven different types of box, so that in theory there was a change of menu for each day of the week. (In practice the "A" box — the one with the steak-and-kydney pudding and the tinned peaches in it — seldom seemed to survive its passage through Base, where it was apt to be swapped for the "F" box, the one with the greasy pork stew and the sad date pudding.)'

'... As the weather was sunny and warm it was no hardship to sleep in the fields around [Rivières]. We dug ourselves in, opened our twenty-four-hour packs, and made ourselves at home. The twenty-four-hour pack ... was a waterproof cardboard box, six inches by five by two-and-a-half, and it contained enough to keep one man's body and soul together for one day. The backbone of the diet was porridge and stew, each compressed into a small iron-hard brick which, when whittled down with a penknife and heated with water, blossomed miraculously into something very like a real meal. Round them were blocks of tea-milk-and-sugar, chocolate, and meat extract; and there were besides boiled sweets, packets of chewing gum, soft unsweetened biscuits, lump sugar, and salt. Each man carried two of these packs and one tin of bully beef; and although some of us were landed a day ahead of schedule and consequently had to exist on the packs for three days instead of two, nearly all of us had some food left by the end of the third day.'

**Capt Alastair Borthwick, 5th Bn,
Seaforth Highlanders,
British 51st Highland Div (1)**

(US National Archives)

'The GI's food came up to the front lines as B-, C-, D- and K-ration packs. If the soldiers were lucky [it] would be prepared by company cooks and brought up in thermal marmite cans. Small squad stoves, 'canned heat' or C2 explosive could also be used to warm rations. Toiletries, tobacco and candy were usually issued free to GIs in the divisional area.

'The B-rations were group canned meals in large quantities — 5-in-1, later 10-in-1 (i.e. five meals for one man or one meal for five men) ... too bulky to carry in combat unless you had a vehicle.

'The D-ration was a 4oz chocolate and wafer bar ... originally designed as an emergency ration. It was intended to taste bad to prevent it being eaten casually; this concept was soon reversed, though to little discernible effect. One veteran described it as "very difficult to eat, hard as a rock and rather bitter ... I would shave it into small fragments to prevent tooth fracture" ...

'The C-ration was originally limited to a range of only three canned meals: stew, hash, and pork and beans. In addition it usually included a D-bar, crackers, hard candy, dextrose (energy) pills, and coffee, cocoa and lemonade mixes. GIs found the [latter] very acidic ... The C-ration pack was heavy (5lbs) and bulky. Its contents were intended to be eaten only for a day or so, but front line GIs often had to eat them for weeks at a time, and rapidly grew to hate them.

'By mid-1943 an accessory/condiment can of cigarettes, gum, toilet paper and water purification tablets (halazone) were added. A spaghetti meal was also added in 1943, and the range was extended until ten meals existed by mid-1944, with hash being dropped; and caramels were substituted for the dextrose pills ...

'The K-ration became available in 1943 and was designed (initially, for paratroops) as an individual combat ration that was easy to carry and consume; two Ks could be carried for every C. They came in breakfast (veal), dinner (spam), and supper (sausage) meals, with condiments, cheese and crackers, candy and gum, drink mixes, toilet paper and smokes. The waxed ration boxes would burn just long enough to heat coffee water ... One veteran's summation was that "... usually the K variety was favored over the C, but both were rather unappetising after weeks of the same."' (2)

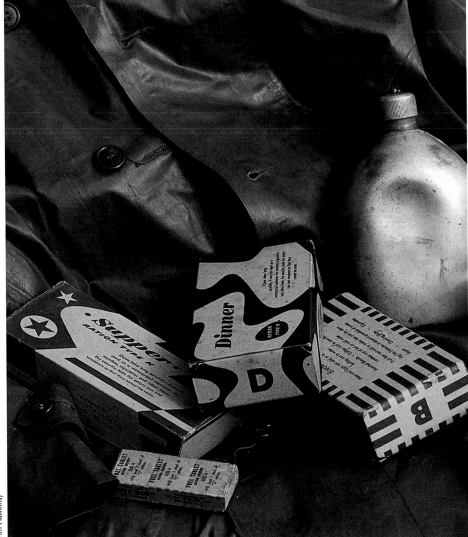

(Tim Hawkins)

The Enemy

Generalisations from Allied soldiers in 1944 — and from veterans since — about the German forces encountered in Normandy vary widely. So did the quality of those forces, in terms of equipment, training, leadership, morale and behaviour.

Given the remorseless demands of the Eastern Front, the divisions garrisoning the thin crust of the 'Atlantic Wall' defences had a low priority. All were weak in numbers — reduced from the 1939 divisional establishment of more than 17,000 to between 11,000 and 13,000 men, often with only six battalions of infantry, and weak in artillery and anti-tank guns. All were short of motor transport, some chronically so, and by Western standards still astonishingly dependent on horses. Some — e.g. the 716th Div, facing the British beaches — were partly composed of 'East-Battalions' of foreigners from German-occupied areas of central Europe and the Soviet Union, usually only too ready to surrender if they got the chance; such troops represented at least 15 per cent of German infantry in France. Some of the German divisions — e.g. the 91st in the Cotentin Peninsula, and the 352nd defending Omaha Beach — were readier to fight, but so chronically lacked vehicles that once the Allies had broken through their initial positions they were unable to manoeuvre and became largely ineffective.

At the other end of the scale, among the reinforcements rushed to the invasion front for the fighting of June-August 1944 were a number of battle-proven divisions which had been stationed in France for rebuilding after suffering heavy casualties on the Russian Front, in Africa and Italy. These sometimes included large numbers of young and inexperienced recruits, but their morale and fitness were correspondingly high — as was their standard of leadership at every level, by cadres who had as much battlefield experience as any soldiers on earth. Formations such as the 2nd and 21st Panzer Divisions, Panzer-Lehr Division, and some of the four Parachute divisions in France were very serious adversaries.

So, notoriously, were the Waffen-SS formations: the 1st 'Leibstandarte Adolf Hitler', 2nd 'Das Reich', 9th 'Hohenstaufen', 10th 'Frundsberg' and 12th 'Hitlerjugend' SS Panzer Divisions, and the 17th SS Panzer-Grenadier Division 'Götz von Berlichingen'. These troops had the best equipment and leadership, were skilled, courageous and highly motivated. Their reputation for ruthlessness on the Eastern Front had gone before them; neither they, nor some of the Allied troops who found themselves confronting the Waffen-SS, were renowned for taking prisoners.

Opinions of the behaviour of, and attitudes towards German troops held by Allied soldiers varied with their personal experiences. These are a just a few of them, recorded both in the heat of battle and on later reflection.

'Each hedgerow presented a formidable obstacle to tanks and offered the ideal in cover and concealment to a fanatically aggressive enemy. Many cases were noted where small groups of enemy left the cover of hedgerows and charged the advancing tanks with hand grenades and anti-tank grenade launchers. This type of opposition rendered our supporting infantry relatively ineffective and caused the tanks to expend enormous quantities of small arms ammunition.'

After Action Report, 2/66th Armd Regt, US 2nd Armd Div — the enemy on this occasion are believed to have been from the 17th SS Pz-Gren Div (1)

'I remember that, just before this, we had passed a pillbox where a 19-year-old German officer had been the only survivor and had been loading and firing the 88mm gun on his own, until shot from behind by the infantry.'

Pte John White, 200 Field Ambulance, British RAMC (2)

'We were not as well armed as the enemy. His tanks were much superior. In the hospital the German soldiers told me they called our tanks "Tommy Torches". His light machine gun, belt fed, in my view was much more effective than the Bren. The German soldier, good as he was, was not that marvellous — he was better armed in the essentials.'

Pte D. Davies, 7th Bn, Hampshire Regt, British 43rd Inf Div (3)

'We came to know the 858th Regiment quite well. Deserters used to drop in to see us nearly every morning, always (to my annoyance, because I was now Intelligence Officer and had to interrogate them) at stand-down. Before long we knew almost as much about the German positions as we did about our own, because deserters as a class are talkative persons and in any case no one in the German Army then or later had the least idea of security. These men who came in were all Poles or Russians, each protesting that he was in the Wehrmacht against his will, and anxious to prove his good faith by giving his friends away down to the last detail. The Russians were unable to do this, because no Russian ever learned to speak anything but Russian, but the Poles were better linguists. They gave our gunners some beautiful targets.'

Capt Alastair Borthwick, 5th Bn, Seaforth Highlanders, British 51st

(Left) Propaganda photograph of a gunner with his pet on the invasion front. German units garrisoning the Atlantic Wall included a number made up of older men or those with low standards of fitness — so-called 'ear and stomach battalions'; e.g. the 709th Inf Div defending Utah Beach had an average age of 36 years. Such troops could, of course, man machine guns and cannon in defensive emplacements with just as lethal effect as teenagers; but once their thin belt of coastal defences was pierced they were effectively destroyed. Mounting successful counter-attacks demands a much higher level of morale and stamina than most of these troops could offer.

(Right) Quad-20mm cannon manned by German paratroopers in Normandy (these anti-aircraft weapons were also used in ground combat). In the 24 hours up to nightfall on D-Day the Allied air forces flew about 14,700 sorties, and lost 127 aircraft (not including gliders), the great majority of them airborne troop transports shot down by German flak. (Luftwaffe fighters played no part in the German resistance; famously, only two Fw190s made a single ineffective pass over the beaches.)

However, during the months-long pre-invasion air campaign to destroy the northern French rail network and seal off the invasion coast some 20,000 Allied aircrew had been lost.

(Left) By contrast to the photo opposite, this portrait of a paratrooper exemplifies one of the best types of soldiers in Normandy. A jump-qualified senior private in his early to mid-twenties, he is identified by his insignia as an NCO candidate with ground combat experience on the Russian Front dating back to 1941/42. Such men were typical of the cadre of Col von der Heydte's 6th Paratroop Regt, 3,500 strong with an average rank-and-file age of less than 18 years, which was one of the few German units to react decisively to the Allied airborne attacks in the early hours of 6 June. Although by 1944 the mass of the Fallschirmjäger regiments were paratroops in name only — i.e. they were never deployed by parachute, being used simply as elite light infantry — the fact that they were volunteers, most of whom had passed jump training, ensured that they were some of the best human material still available to the much-diminished Wehrmacht.

'I went round the wounded and made a list of priorities for operation. The list consisted mainly of "abdominals". The German and British wounded were all lying together. I came to one young, very young German, lying between two British. "No, don't bother with me," he said. "Take those two first." He died, in fact, before his turn came for operation.'

Mr J. M. Leggate, FRCS, British RAMC (5)

'Snipers were at their worst. Maj. Young's Coy was clearing some farm buildings [when a] shot whistled uncomfortably close. Maj. Y. turned to Pte. Lace (Bn sniper) with "That's the fifth shot that basket has fired at me, we must get him." They found him hidden in a junk-heap in the middle of a duck pond! They found another not more than seventeen years old, who had buried himself in the mud of a wet ditch ... Another was burned out of a hayrick set on fire by a German shell. Several days after, snipers were still being found. One had barricaded himself in a room on the first floor of a barn while a platoon of D Coy occupied the ground floor. They got him out with a Bren gun burst fired through the closed door when he refused to come.'

Capt Marshall, 7th Bn, Somerset Light Infantry, British 43rd Inf Div (6)

'Practically everybody was out on patrol every night to give the impression that we were very strong, which we were not, and to keep the enemy off balance. It is easy to knock the German off his stride. He is a great book man, very well organised, but if you disorganise him he finds it hard to reorganise. You have got to keep hitting him, not necessarily cause many casualties, just keep at them.'

Lt Col Alastair Pearson, 8th Parachute Bn, British 6th Abn Div (7)

'Hitler's gunmen are "supermen" in many ways. There is no monkey business about them. It has been drilled into them for years that instantaneous and absolutely unquestioning obedience is the thing; but they do not react that way as prisoners. They have nothing but scornful contempt for the Joes in charge of them. They can't understand mercy. If some kindly GI Joe hands out a package of cigarettes or a chocolate bar — the Krauts think he's a sucker.'

Lt Paul Unger, Military Police, US 2nd Armd Div, in a letter to his family (8)

(Simon Pugh-Jones)

'We had captured a bunch of Germans ... earlier all wearing green uniforms. These [latest] prisoners that came out of the bomb shelter were wearing dark blue or black uniforms with [Waffen-SS] lightning streaks on the right lapel ... It was the first time we had seen uniforms like this ... I called the company commander via radio and said, "We have 17 prisoners, where do you want them?" He called back a few minutes later and gave us map coordinates to a location not far ahead [where we were to] turn the prisoners over to a French Underground group ... We left the 17 POWs with the French as we had been instructed ... Later I received a radio message from some MPs, inquiring where I had dropped off prisoners. I gave them the map coordinates ... These MPs verified it was the right place and asked, "Can you identify the prisoners you dropped off?" I said, "All I know is that they were wearing dark uniforms with lightning streaks on their collars." He came back, "Well, we have 17 people laying down here on the ground and their throats are cut from ear to ear."'

Sgt Charles Rost, 67th Armd Regt, US 2nd Armd Div (9)

'The night before the attack at La Varinière was a bad one for the Bn, shelling was particularly severe and many casualties resulted. Jerry was getting desperate now. We had no sleep that night but still the next day ... we were to spearhead the breakout. B Coy's strength after this attack dwindled to only twenty-eight. This was one of my better days, for some reason I was not afraid, any other time I was almost petrified with fear and I don't mind admitting it. My Platoon Commander was badly wounded, that upset me. My anger was very real.

'Afterward Hoppy said, "I thought you were going to kill those prisoners when you wanted them to run." But for his calming influence I may have done just that: I was in no mood for messing about.'

Pte. Albert Kings, Bren gunner, 1st Bn, Worcestershire Regt, British 43rd Inf Div (10)

The 12th SS Panzer Division 'Hitlerjugend' was raised in June 1943 from 18-year-old former Hitler Youth members, led by officers and NCOs from the premier Waffen-SS division, the 1st Pz Div 'Leibstandarte Adolf Hitler'. This was a formidable combination; young, inexperienced soldiers with high morale and experienced leaders make the best infantry. (There is a fine line between combat experience and war-weariness, as some of the veteran British and American units from Africa and the Mediterranean, and some German units from the Russian Front, would demonstrate in summer 1944.) The first SS troops to confront the invaders, elements of 'HJ' went into action west of Caen early on 7 June. On 8 June regimental commander Col Kurt 'Panzer' Meyer — who took over divisional command a week later — is believed to have ordered the killing of some 45 Canadian prisoners (not the last to be murdered by this division). The 'HJ' and the Canadians fought each other thereafter with merciless determination during the four-week struggle for Caen, and the SS division was virtually wiped out by the end of August.

'I believe [the Germans] were unquestionably the best army in the world. They fought with great skill. Their use of ground was remarkable. Their ability to plugs gaps by junior commanders taking the initiative, without waiting for orders from on high was far superior to ours. Much later, when the German army had been defeated in France, pulled back over the Seine and chased into Holland and Belgium, they were able to produce a cohesive defence against us by bringing in remnants of batteries, regiments and battalions. They formed battle groups on an ad hoc basis to produce a swift and resolute defence. If the German Army had not been bled white in the East, and continued to be engaged by the Russians, I do not know how we would have defeated them.'

Capt Freddie Graham, in 1944 IO, 2nd Bn, Argyll & Sutherland Highlanders, British 15th Scottish Div (11)

'... It has become the custom ... to extol the professional ability of the Wehrmacht whilst decrying that of our own fighting arms, particularly our armour and infantry. This has perplexed me because it runs contrary to my experience. My 18 Platoon were better soldiers than any we fought. So was D Company and the whole 4th Battalion, The Somerset Light Infantry ...

'Although they lost, the German soldiers ... are proud of their exploits, many of which were considerable. It is, of course, very much in their own interest to encourage the theory and myth that, although superior as fighting men, they were beaten only by numerically superior forces and firepower. In my experience this was not so. In many attacks the prisoners we took outnumbered our attacking force and German units who would continue to resist at close quarters were few indeed. Unlike us, they rarely fought at night, when they were excessively nervous and unsure of themselves. Where we patrolled extensively, they avoided it. I can remember only one successful German patrol and not one successful night action. If our positions had been reversed, I doubt if they would have performed better than we did. Without doubt, some Wehrmacht formations were extremely professionally competent but many were not. Some of the enemy infantry fought with fanaticism but most did not.'

Lt Sydney Jary, infantry platoon commander in British 43rd Inf Div, July 1944-May 1945 (12)

Wehrmacht prisoners taken by British 43rd Inf Div, and (below) Canadian 3rd Inf Div, during the fighting of July. Most prisoners seemed simply relieved to have survived; those from the 'East-Battalions' were positively enthusiastic at the prospect of captivity. By the end of August many German prisoners displayed signs of being traumatised by prolonged exposure to the very strong and effective Allied artillery, and — though to a lesser extent — by the constant daytime threat of air attack. The accuracy of rocket and bomb attacks by fighter-bombers on individual targets was greatly exaggerated, but road convoys were extremely vulnerable to strafing, and the Allies' complete control of the air was very damaging to German morale. (IW B8315; & National Archives of Canada PA116543/Ken Bell)

(Left) After an encounter battle in the *bocage*, a Tommy from the Durham Light Infantry, 50th Inf Div, bandages a wounded signals NCO from a German Army motorised unit. In battle it was often difficult to get one's surrender accepted — there were too many ambiguous situations, and the universal rule was 'better safe than sorry'. Once the heat of combat had cooled most ordinary soldiers on both sides treated prisoners decently. The similarity of the ordeal they had shared was so obvious that a submissive attitude often attracted the basic gestures of a drink of water, a handful of food or a cigarette. The main exceptions involved Waffen-SS troops, and other individuals who were foolish enough to show arrogance towards captors who were still in the grip of the fever of battle. (IWM B5525)

The American Front

(Tim Hawkins)

'Our real baptism of fire came three days later, and on June 9 heavy enemy fire tore our unit apart. All the officers were killed and the rest of us struggled on for about a month with sergeants in command.'
Pte Anthony Jele, 1st Bn, 8th Inf Regt, US 4th Inf Div (1)

'They'd talked about the hedgerows, but they hadn't told us about French hedgerows ... We'd practised in England, and the hedgerows that grow in England are about two feet six high and a foot thick, and you can just shove your way through and there's no big deal. But it's not so in Normandy, there are all these little fields with a mound of earth about three feet high and then there's the hedge growing out of that, and trees growing out of it, and there's a great drainage ditch at the bottom, so you could literally be dying in one field, and in the next field people would be taking a break and having a smoke and never know anything about you.'
Lt Henry Lefebvre, A Co, 508th PIR, US 82nd Abn Div (2)

'As soon as we got to the top of the crest off the beach we immediately found that French hedgerows were different. In France, the hedgerow was a mound of dirt from six to ten or twelve feet high with heavy hedges on top and roots that worked down into the mounds, and the mounds themselves were very effective barriers. You simply could not pass through a hedgerow. You had to climb up something and then at the top you were practically blocked by the jungle of plant roots and trunks, vines, branches ...

'The Germans would dig into the back of a hedgerow, put a machine-gun nest in there, and then cut a very small slit looking forward, providing them with a field of fire with what was for practical purposes absolute protection. You couldn't see them as they fired.'
Capt John C. Raaen, US 5th Ranger Bn (3)

US Infantry advancing cautiously up the ditch at the foot of a hedgerow near St Lô, mid-July 1944. (US National Archives)

(Simon Pugh-Jones)

At least one man in each infantry squad carried the Browning Automatic Rifle, with 20-round magazines. Lt Sidney Salomon of the 2nd Ranger Bn recalled that while in training in the USA nobody wanted to carry the BAR, because of the extra weight — 'but once we got in combat, everybody wanted one, for the firepower.'

'When our men appeared, laboriously working their way forward, the Germans could knock off the first one or two, cause the others to duck down behind the bank, and then call for his own mortar support. The German mortars were very, very efficient. By the time our men were ready to go after him, the German and his men and his guns had obligingly retired to the next stop. If our men had rushed him instead of ducking behind the bank, his machine-gun or machine-pistol would knock a number off. It was what you might call in baseball parlance, a fielder's choice. No man was very enthusiastic about it. But back in the dugout I have often heard the remark in tones of contempt and anger: "Why don't they get up and go?"'

Anonymous US infantry officer (4)

'We got an urgent call to support the 101st [Airborne Division, who] had landed by parachute on D-Day and were holding anchor between Omaha and Utah Beaches, which hinged on the little town of Carentan. We were told that the 101st was under heavy counterattack and urgently in need of all the support we could give them. I got into Carentan and found that the condition of the 101st had not been exaggerated. They were down to about 30 per cent strength, with very little medical support, getting low on food, but just as cocky as ever.'

Lt Col John S. Wier, 48th Medical Bn, US 2nd Armd Div (5)

A squad following a tank along a typical sunken lane, D+4. It was natural to take advantage of the cover of the high banks, but this channelled movement in ways predictable by the waiting enemy. The normal infantry tactics of 'fire and movement' — squads leapfrogging one another, alternately dashing forward and giving covering fire — were extraordinarily difficult to apply in this sort of terrain.
(US National Archives)

(Simon Pugh-Jones)

(Right) A tired sergeant of the 4th Inf Div takes a smoke break in the *bocage*. The papers stowed inside his helmet are probably letters from home. (US National Archives)

(US National Archives)

'At 3:00 sharp, a fierce rumbling shook the road — big, beautiful Shermans of the 2nd Armored Division came roaring with armored infantrymen trailing them, men fresh from the beaches and spoiling for a fight. The tank leaders spotted Fox Company's line and fanned out in front. Those equipped with bulldozer plows crashed through hedgerows as if they were soft paper, permitting others to race through. It was wonderful to watch them at work and many retired to higher ground, the better to watch them. A tank would stop in a hole made by a brother tank dozer, then turn a sharp right or left, wherever the Krauts were, and sweep every foot of the hedgerow. When and what they missed were mopped up and destroyed by the armored infantrymen. The men were treated to an awe inspiring show of violence and destruction of the first order. The enemy dissolved before the calm, deliberate fury of this 2nd Armored unit.'

Stan Myers, F Co, 506th PIR, US 101st Abn Div (6)

'I again saw the wreckage of war — the dead and dying lying in the fields around Carentan, friend and enemy side by side. We found anywhere from 2 to 50 in each little field of probably less than an acre and there were lots of fields. We gave any paratrooper that came to our tank a belt of .30 caliber from our machine guns. The weary paratroopers had been fighting for a week, and they were down to fighting with bayonets and knives. These men had seen hundreds of enemy and also buddies killed with little or no emotion, yet several of them broke down and cried when they got those shells. We kept moving between Carentan and Catz, dodging SSs and artillery shells constantly, until moving back to our original spot at Blay about 8pm on the 17th.'

Staff Sergeant Gatzke, 66th Armd Regt, US 2nd Armd Div (7)

'Being shelled is the real work of an infantry soldier, which no one talks about. Everyone has his own way of going about it. In general, it means lying face down and contracting your body into as small a space as possible. In novels you read about soldiers, at such moments, fouling themselves. The opposite is true. As all your parts are contracting, you are more likely to be constipated.'

Pte Louis Simpson, US 101st Abn Div (8)

'The people who do the actual advancing to close with the enemy are the rifle platoons ... The battles progress no faster than they do. Now the aggregate strength of these 81 platoons [in each Infantry Division] is about 3,240 men. I hazard a guess that at least 75 per cent of the total casualties were in the rifle platoons, or a total of about 2,950 ... This figure is 90 per cent of the rifle platoon strength.'

Anonymous infantry officer, US 30th Inf Div (9)

(Tim Hawkins)

Street fighting in the village of Saintenay on the Carentan/Perriers road, 11 July 1944. Old Norman buildings are solidly built of stone, offering good cover. The Germans fortified both isolated farms and the row (terraced) houses of village streets, and despite the Allies' plentiful artillery and air support the only way to take them was, ultimately, by infantry assault. (US National Archives)

'The terrain over which this action was fought made the execution of a coordinated tank battalion-infantry battalion attack impossible, so that the action consisted of a series of concerted attacks by groups ... no larger than a platoon, with each hedgerow, each field, each sunken road an objective to be taken, mopped up, and secured, before the advance could be continued ...

After Action Report, 2/66th Armd Regt, US 2nd Armd Div (10)

'On the sloping rise of the road appeared the dim outline of a large bush, moving hesitantly and slowly up the road, followed by other indistinct moving objects ... I carried tracer ammunition in my M-1 rifle as did my noncoms. The engineers could tell by the flight and bounce of my tracers if the looming camouflaged bush was armor or not. I quickly fired two clips ... Tracers had hit the thick steel gun shield and were flying in all directions as if spewed from a Roman candle ... The object we laid bare ... was a self-propelled gun ... A large number of vehicles and other equipment followed it.

'As the enemy's leading elements came into ... range, we opened up. Then mortars and automatic weapons joined the battle. Shells crashed in on the unsuspecting Germans in an exploding hailstorm of steel.

'The firing was continuous and concentrated ... There was sporadic answering fire at the outset, which caused most of the casualties to our troops. Three of our engineers were killed ... Pfc Scenna made a one-man attack over a low hedge to try to stem a concentrated attack on our thin line. He was shot at short range as he leaped over the hedge with a scream of defiance. He died with this cry of defiance frozen on his countenance.'

Lt John Wong, C Co, 238th Engineer Combat Bn, US 2nd Armd Div (11)

'Our CCA [Combat Command A] attacked the Germans with the utmost savagery ... we hit [them] with artillery, tanks, and supporting infantry. I do not think they had any idea that there was a unit of such strength anywhere near them. We had taken six prisoners and counted eight hundred Germans killed. Our losses had been minimal. According to reports we got from prisoners throughout the war, from that day on, the Second Armored was a marked division as far as the Germans were concerned. We were greatly hated and greatly feared, and known as "Roosevelt's Butchers" because of the ferocity of our attack.'

Lt Col John S. Weir, 48th Medical Bn, US 2nd Armd Div (12)

(Simon Pugh-Jones)

Street fighting on the outskirts of the port of Brest, where a garrison of German paratroopers held out into September. House-to-house fighting was a deadly game of hide-and-seek, with the initial advantage all on the side of the defender, who would only reveal himself by firing. If stubbornly defended, houses had to be captured floor by floor, room by room, with grenade, rifle and Tommy gun; some-times attackers blasted their way in with bazookas or satchel charges. Even when successful such small-scale combats nearly always cost a squad one or two casualties. Over weeks of fighting the cumulative losses were very heavy; US units were kept in action for long periods, and combat replacements arrived individually. This system was bad for small unit morale: the 'old' soldiers resented the newcomers taking the places of their dead buddies, and the confused replacements often had no chance to settle in and learn combat skills before they themselves became casualties. By the end of the August fighting many rifle platoons had only a handful of the men left who had landed on D-Day.
(US National Archives)

The camouflage uniforms issued experimentally in July to the 2nd Armd Div and the 30th Inf Div were dangerously similar in appearance to the camouflage clothing worn by Waffen-SS troops, leading to a number of tragic mistakes. They were withdrawn after a few weeks. (US National Archives)

'Many members of the [2nd Armored] division had been wearing the same gas-impregnated olive-drab wool shirts and pants (ODs) or green herring-bone twill (HBT) fatigues since landing in France. By now they were getting pretty ripe. Most companies of the 41st AIR [Armored Infantry Regt] and the 17th Armored Engineer Battalion received new two-piece HBT camouflage suits on an organizational basis. Individuals going to divisional supply at this time were also issued the camo suits separately. It appears that these units, along with elements of the 30th Infantry Division, were the only American troops in the ETO to be issued the camouflage clothing. Mainly because of the many problems that arose from wearing these suits in battle zones, they were recalled from use before the end of August, never to be issued again in the ETO ...

'Returning from a patrol through the lines of the 4th Infantry Division clad in a camouflaged suit, [Lawrence E. "Chubby" Williams] was fired upon by a machine gun post manned by Ivy Division soldiers ... In one attack that summer, Staff Sergeant Ralph Darr of A/41st was [wearing a camouflage suit and] walking in front of a 67th AR tank, which fired a burst of machine gun fire at him. A bullet glanced off his helmet, knocking him down ... He ran to the phone on the rear of the tank and said, "Why don't you guys stick your heads outside of these tanks and see what you're shooting at, once in a while?" (13)

'When we returned to the headquarters area, a [soldier] had killed a German by beating him to death with his carbine. We asked why he didn't shoot him and he said, "I forgot." The young fellow also wanted to know if he would have to pay for the gun he smashed. We assured him he didn't.

'General Brooks arrived ... he wanted me to express his pride to the remainder of the command ... At that very moment someone behind us let loose with a tommy gun and sprayed the tree right in front of [us]. Brooks looked at me and said, "I just told you I'm proud of you people, but you're getting trigger happy. Now you get that stopped." I started to say, "yes sir," when out of that tree fell the deadest German you will ever see.'

Capt Jack Hart, 78th Armd Field Arty Bn, US 2nd Armd Div (14)

(Tim Hawkins)

'The enemy we faced were a mixed lot of survivors of the bombing plus newly arrived paratroopers. The dead from both sides lay twisted and torn, some half buried by overturned earth. Many Germans were still in shock from the bombing and many had no desire at all to fight ... I don't see how any of them even survived. Bomb craters big enough to swallow a jeep were so close together in some areas it was difficult for our tank drivers to zigzag through. Our tank company was wonderfully aggressive, shooting up everything in sight. The tank commander's tactics were very sensible ... Since no Americans were ahead of him, his orders were to shoot and shoot. All that tank firepower blasting away kept the enemy pinned ... unable to return fire, and allowed us to advance rapidly and capture many prisoners with very few losses'.

Lt George Wilson, 22nd Inf Regt, US 4th Inf Div (15)

'The road had a high bank on each side. The German soldiers were marching in columns on both sides of the road. We caught them with artillery and machine gun fire. I have never seen so many dead in all my life. Some were still leaning on the bank and looked like they were still alive. I saw the infantry boys go over and shake them to see if they were alive. Trees were blown down, and many cows and horses were killed. I remember pulling into a field, and getting out of my tank and sitting on a log. I said aloud, "I believe everything and everybody but us is dead."'

William L. Rape, 2nd Armd Div (16)

Sherman tanks advancing past a shot-up German horse-drawn convoy. Many Wehrmacht divisions still relied on horses for their supply columns and even their artillery; and in the Falaise Pocket the large numbers of dead horses added to the repulsive stench of the hot summer battlefield, which all veterans recalled.
(US National Archives)

Medics from the US 35th Inf Div examine a dead German soldier. Once again, the man at left has an apparent 'beer belly' from stowing gear inside his jacket rather than carry his pack into combat. (US National Archives)

'About 0730, after daylight, the company started coming out of the woodwork, looking sort of sheepish. 1st Sgt Menker and I went on a little recon. Down the road we found a German column... looks like the lead vehicle had broken down and the rest had tailgated up against it. This is where the artillery caught them. I feel sure that there were at least 150 dead Germans in and around those vehicles. The artillerymen had to cut their powder load to half to lob shells that close to them.'

Sgt H. V. Robinson, 1st Bn, 41st Armd Inf Regt, US 2nd Armd Div (17)

'You could not see the sleeping men, but you could hear them. Few snored, but there was much whimpering and moaning, as in a hospital ward. Occasionally one would cry out or mumble a few incoherent words ... But the worst sound was of men grinding their teeth as they slept. You could not see them, but you could hear them and smell them, too. Wet clothing and sweat and the rank smell of dirty wet feet and urine ... They had got out their wounded and got in ammunition and cold rations. But they weren't ... doing all the folderol that the book prescribed, because they had had three days of hard fighting and they were exhausted. They pitched into the places the Germans had left and they slept, for tomorrow they had to go ahead again.' (18)

Exhausted GIs from the 120th Inf Regt, 20th Inf Div are interrupted by an Army photographer while trying to catch some sleep in a wine cellar at Tessey-sur-Vire, 3 August 1944. (US National Archives)

Air Support

B-17G Flying Fortress bombers of the US 8th Army Air Force. The USAAF and RAF heavy bomber force was withdrawn from its strategic bombing programme over Germany in the run-up to D-Day and was committed to attacks along the invasion coast. These were of very mixed value. The degree of accuracy needed to bomb the coastal defences was seldom achieved, though where hits were made on German bunkers they caused massive damage. In late July the Allied command used 'carpet bombing' of the German front lines to break the stalemate and blast paths for armoured break-throughs (e.g. Operation 'Cobra'), but again with mixed results. In the Cotentin the sectors held by the Panzer-Lehr Div and 13th & 15th Parachute Regts were devastated.

'The company had been hit directly by our bombs. Their casualties ... were heavy. Men went to pieces and had to be sent back. The company was shattered and shaking. And yet B Company attacked on time, to the minute! (forty minutes after our heavy bombing had ceased). They attacked and within an hour sent back word that they had advanced 800 yards through German territory and were still going. Around our farmyard, men with stars on their shoulders almost wept ... The American soldier can be majestic when he needs to be.'

War correspondent Ernie Pyle, with the US 4th Inf Div (1)

(Below) 8th US Army Air Force P-51D Mustang fighter painted with D-Day black/white recognition stripes. The Allies' complete dominance of the air over Normandy kept Luftwaffe attacks on the Allied armies rare and in weak strength. The fighter-bombers — USAAF Mustangs and P-47 Thunderbolts and RAF Typhoons and Spitfires — were a scourge to the Germans, making all daytime troop movements dangerous. Although their unguided rockets and bombs did not score many hits on individually dispersed tanks, they could reduce large targets like road convoys to charnel-houses.

On the other hand, the Allied system of ground/air communications was not yet efficient enough to allow pinpoint control of air strikes. Many hundreds of Allied lives were lost to 'friendly fire' from above during the Normandy fighting; it was simply too difficult for a fighter pilot to distinguish friend from foe.

'... The 5th Camerons had had to abandon their attack ... because the Spitfires had knocked out every wireless vehicle they possessed and they were unable to communicate with Brigade, their companies, or the gunners. Against such an emergency we had each been provided with a triangle of bright yellow silk, the idea being that the forward troops should lay them out and draw attention to themselves. The triangles, however, were by no means foolproof, because the man who was being shot up was usually much too busy taking cover to have time to display one; whereas all the troops a mile behind him, fearing that they would be the next victims, immediately rushed to display theirs. The pilot then took these triangles to be the front line and continued to harry those in front — if he saw the triangles at all, which ... was doubtful.'

**Capt Alastair Borthwick,
5th Bn, Seaforth Highlanders,
British 51st Highland Div (2)**

(US National Archive)

(US National Archives)

Tanks in the Bocage

(Below) Column of camouflaged M4 Shermans of the US 70th Tank Bn negotiating a narrow Normandy road, July 1944. (US Army)

On paper the Allies enjoyed a considerable advantage in tank numbers over the Germans. In fact the relative quality of the available tank types, and the terrain of the Normandy *bocage*, tipped the balance in favour of the Panzer commanders for much of the battle — facts of which the Allied tank crews were only too aware.

Classic tank tactics resembled the infantry's 'fire and movement' — tanks, troops (of four or five tanks) or squadrons (of three or four troops) advanced alternately, covering each other by firing from 'hull-down positions' in which only the heavily armoured front of the gun turret was exposed. Good tank country for attackers was open, rolling countryside allowing fast, flexible cross-country movement but affording concealment behind ripples in the terrain. The *bocage* was the absolute opposite of this: broken into small fields by high banked hedgerows, copses and sunken lanes, it hindered and channelled movement, cut visibility, and provided countless defensive ambush positions from which individual German tanks and self-propelled guns could inflict heavy casualties before withdrawing to the next.

The standard US and British tank was the Sherman; the British also had some Churchills and Cromwells. In terms of armour protection and firepower they were comparable with the most numerous German type, the elderly but up-rated PzKw IV; but they were completely outclassed by the PzKw V Panther and PzKw VI Tiger, both of which had guns able to penetrate Allied tank armour at ranges far beyond the effective reach of the Allied tank guns. To destroy a Panther or Tiger meant getting close up — within a very few hundred yards — and firing at its thinner side or rear armour; the massive frontal armour was virtually invulnerable. It was said that to destroy a Tiger in tank-vs.-tank combat would cost three Shermans destroyed before a fourth could get close enough.

The Allied crews suffered from a 'Tiger psychosis': they automatically assumed that any German tank they encountered was a Tiger, and the quotations which follow illustrate this. In fact there were only three weak battalions of Tigers in Normandy at various times during the battle, totalling perhaps 80 tanks at their peak, and half that number by August.

The Normandy hedgerows were overcome to some extent by the ingenuity of an American sergeant named Cullin, who had the idea of cutting up German beach obstacles to make giant teeth and welding them to the bows of tanks so that they could plough straight through the banks. Both US and British units quickly adopted these 'Cullin Devices', illustrated here on an M4A1 76mm Sherman at Pont Hebert in July. They were normally removed after the Allies got out of the *bocage* country. (US Army)

There were seldom many more than about 300 Panthers. There were perhaps 1,100 PzKw IVs; their added external kit of spaced armour plates gave them something of the boxy shape of the much larger Tiger, and this encouraged mistaken identification in the heat of battle (a mistake still frequently made by writers of photo captions).

Despite these advantages, the Panzer units were usually understrength when they arrived on the battlefield and were quickly 'written down'. For instance, the theoretical strength of SS Pz Regt 12 in the 'Hitlerjugend' Div was 101 PzKw IVs and 81 Panthers, or 182 tanks in all. Its actual strength in June was 91 plus 48, or 139 tanks; and by 8 July it had just 32 PzKw IVs and 24 Panthers, or 56 tanks. Similarly, the German Army's crack Panzer-Lehr Div had a theoretical strength of 103 PzKw IVs plus 79 Panthers and a squadron of 14 Tigers — 196 tanks. It never achieved anything like that figure; and by 1 August it had just 15 PzKw IVs and 12 Panthers left.

The terrain made it difficult for the advancing Allies to bring conventional anti-tank guns into action, and anyway

(cont. overleaf)

Knocked-out PzKw V ('Mk V') Panther burning in a Normandy orchard on 27 June during the British Operation 'Epsom' west of Caen. Tests with 75mm Sherman guns showed that even the Panther's thinner side armour could not be penetrated at over 800 yards, and the front was invulnerable at 150 yards. The Panther's more powerful long 75mm gun could defeat the frontal armour of a Sherman at 1,000 yards, that of a British Churchill at 800 yards, and their side or rear armour at 2,800 and 2,000 yards respectively. Allied tank men were driven to discussing desperate tricks like ricocheting shells up off the ground in front in the hope of penetrating the thinner belly, or aiming low on the gun mantlet to glance down through the lighter roof plates. A few extraordinary gunners managed these feats, but few crews had such marksmanship or blind luck. (IWM B6055)

(cont from page 91)

their 57mm and 6-pounder types were inferior to the large German tank guns. However, the close country favoured infantry tank-killer teams. The Germans had two main infantry AT weapons which were used with great effect from close range ambush positions. The *Panzerschreck*, a direct copy of the US bazooka, was an electrically fired, shoulder-held tube for launching rocket projectiles. The revolutionary *Panzerfaust* was the ancestor of today's 'use-and-throw-away' shoulder-fired AT rockets, with a powerful shaped charge warhead. US infantry had the bazooka, and the British and Canadians the PIAT (Projector Infantry Anti-Tank)— a powerful but awkward weapon which had to be manually cocked.

One of the great lessons of the Normandy fighting was the mutual dependence of tank crews and infantry. The tanks could blast machine gun nests which held up the infantry, but needed foot soldiers to spot the enemy tank-killer teams stalking them under cover.

(Tim Hawkins)

'The standard tank crew consisted of five men, the commander, driver, assistant driver, gunner and loader-operator ... Imagine these men crammed into a pre-1942 automobile to appreciate the amount of space within. The cannon would be poking out the center of the windshield. One of the two .30 caliber machine guns would be thrusting from the area of the glove compartment. A ring mount .50 caliber machine gun is where the sunroof would be. The sides and the rear of the car would be encircled with 75 mm cannon shells, neatly stowed within reach of the gunners ... The driver's window is like looking out the mail slot in your front door. There are aiming devices and periscopes to be used when the tank is buttoned up for battle. Your car would be filled with engine fumes, smoke from expended shells, odors from sweaty bodies, and the dust ... from the battlefield. On the exterior of the tank was a fluorescent panel draped over the rear deck, which was already crammed with lashed down camouflage nets, ration boxes, extra jerrycans of fuel, water cans, bedrolls, and other necessities. The GIs riding piggyback on the rear deck hang on by their fingernails, always mindful of the German Panzerfaust, incoming 88mm shells, of being swept off as the big gun tube traverses, or of falling off and being crushed by the following tank.'

Lt John Wong, 238th Engineer Combat Bn, US 2nd Armd Div (1)

(Tim Hawkins)

'... Attached to [our battalion] were a company of seventeen Sherman tanks and a platoon of tank destroyers ... By nightfall, nine of the seventeen tanks would be demolished and the infantry would be almost wiped out. Our ruination was the famous German 88, the incredible 88 mm artillery piece. A direct hit did not bounce off the sloping four inch solid steel armor plate front of a Sherman tank; it went clear through and out the back. I saw smoking tanks ripped through from front to back by a single armor-piercing 88. Rarely did any of the crew survive, for along with the shell were the ricocheting chunks of tank metal it tore off, not to mention the inevitable concussion and internal bleeding. Fire also made it difficult to rescue the wounded, as shells inside exploded from the heat. Tanks were often deathtraps for the crew.'

Lt George Wilson, 22nd Inf Regt,
US 4th Inf Div (2)

(Tim Hawkins)

(Below) GIs slog down the road to St Lô during the July fighting, past a wrecked Panther. It lies in a large crater, and the turret has been completely blown off; it is therefore almost certainly a victim of air force 'carpet bombing'. Only the 17-pounder-gun British 'Firefly' conversion of the Sherman could take on a Panther with any confidence even at 600 yards, and there were only enough Fireflies to issue one per troop of four Shermans. However, once the war moved out of the *bocage* into the more open fighting of autumn 1944 it became clear that the level of tactical skill in the Panzer units had deteriorated markedly through the heavy losses among experienced crews, and Shermans often took on equal numbers of Panthers successfully - the Allied tank commanders and gunners were simply quicker and more accurate.
(US National Archives)

Two Tommies from 49th Inf Div enjoy a rare sight: a wrecked PzKw VI Tiger. Generally Tigers were only present in the ranks of three small Heavy Tank Battalions deployed at corps level. Despite their small actual numbers, the threat of the Tigers' massive 88mm guns — effective against the thickest Allied tank armour at 1,000 yards, and against much of it at more than twice that range — gave all Allied tank crews nightmares, and they routinely misidentified less powerful adversaries as Tigers. The 60-ton Tiger could sometime be destroyed by Shermans if 'stalked' through cover to very close range and shot up from the flank or rear. (IWM B6140)

'The [Sherman] tank's top speed varied with the kind of engine fitted, and could be as low as 20mph or as high as 30. It weighed 30 tons. Some Shermans were fitted in British factories with 17-pounder anti-tank guns, replacing the 75mm ... [which] could not penetrate the heavy [German tanks] at all, while the German 88mm, or long 75mm, could not fail to knock out a Sherman at almost any range — certainly 2,000 yards. The 17-pounder was capable of knocking out a Tiger or Panther at a moderate range, and was comparable to the German guns, but the Sherman was still at a disadvantage because of its much inferior armour.

'Anti-tank shot does not depend on an explosion to penetrate a tank's armour. An ordinary HE shell would not affect a Sherman, unless it was very large ... The armour-piercing projectile's effectiveness depends largely on velocity. The damage inside a tank is caused by the projectile tearing through, and by flying fragments of armour spraying around inside ... A petrol-engined Sherman would almost always catch fire because of the vapour inside. The tremendous impact of the projectile on armour would generate tremendous heat, producing something very like an explosion.'
Tpr Austin Baker,
4th/7th Royal Dragoon Guards,
British 8th Armd Bde (3)

The Germans deployed large numbers of self-propelled ('SP') guns — turretless tanks with powerful guns mounted in low, sloping, fixed superstructures. Cheaper to produce than tanks, these were just as effective in the defensive fighting which characterised the battle for Normandy. Note also the similarity of this SS camouflage clothing with that experimentally issued to some US units — see page 85.

(Tim Hawkins)

British Shermans of the 2nd Fife & Forfar Yeomanry, 11th Armd Div, near Cheux on 25 June during one of the very costly battles west of Caen. A German gun has just scored a direct hit on an ammunition truck coming forward to re-arm the tanks. (IWM B6017)

'I have fired at 150 yards at a Panther, 6 rounds — 4 APs and 2 HEs, without penetration'.
Staff sergeant, US 2nd Armd Div (4)

'We had orders to take up position in the front of Maltot in D Coy area facing the German side of Hill 112. This was open for tank warfare in places. Six Churchill tanks coming up through Maltot set off across country to a wood. They were all knocked out like skittles by a Jerry 88 mm gun which was in a copse under cover. It could have been tanks or anti-tank guns but they really massacred our tanks. The German 88 mm easily outgunned our 6-pounder A/Tk guns, starting off at about 1,000 yards. Our effective range was only 400 yards and our 17-pounder never seemed far enough forward to engage them.'
Sgt Reg Romain, AT Ptn, 5th Bn, Wiltshire Regt, British 43rd Inf Div (5)

'I have personally observed on a number of occasions the projectiles fired by our 75mm and 76mm guns bouncing off the front plate of Mark V tanks [Panthers] at ranges of about 600 yards'.
Col Maurice Rose, US 2nd Armd Div (4)

'The only Panthers I have seen not knocked out by our artillery or our air, were either abandoned by their crews or had been hit by our tanks at very close ranges ... We defeat the German tanks by our weight in sheer numbers of tanks and men.'
Lt Col E. W. Blanchard, US 3rd Armd Div (4)

'At dusk, enemy tanks closed in on Point 103. Shermans were blazing everywhere. Going to the Brigadier's tank, I was hailed by the CO of 24th Lancers, sitting on the ground, with his arm in a sling. He handed me his rifle, saying, "Put a round in the breech, at least I'll take one of them with me." I thought, "Good God, it's as bad as that is it?" Shortly after, all firing ceased. It was the final attempt by the enemy, before pulling out and leaving St Pierre.'

Maj Peter Martin, 151 Inf Bde, British 50th Inf Div (6)

(Tim Hawkins)

US 3rd Army GIs riding Shermans into the front line during Gen Patton's sweep into Brittany following the break-out achieved by Operation 'Cobra' in the last week of July. Riding tanks was neither comfortable nor safe, but it was preferable to walking. The turret gave an illusion of shelter, but in fact tanks drew enemy fire. (US National Archives)

Camouflaged anti-tank gun crew of the 12th SS Pz Div 'Hitlerjugend' in Normandy. This fanatical division of teenage Nazis, led by battle-hardened veterans from the Eastern Front, had taken 60 per cent casualties by the time Caen fell on 9 July. Further mauled by Canadian and Polish units in the Falaise battles, the division was reduced to about 600 men with no tanks by the time it was withdrawn to Germany at the end of August. This represented about 95 per cent casualties since early June.

'The regimental [rendezvous] initially consisted of precisely nine tanks out of the sixty or so that had started in the morning. Gradually others came in, but the losses had been very heavy. Nobody said very much, except things like, "You know so-and-so's had it." The surviving reserve crews brought up spare tanks, and the whole night was spent replenishing, re-organising, repairing, and getting set for the next day. Once more, sleep did not figure on the programme.'

Lt Steel Brownlie, 2nd Fife & Forfar Yeomanry, British 11th Armd Div (7)

'The tank in front of my armoured car was hit by a Panzerfaust and the assistant driver was killed; the front of his head was sliced off by the shell and the periscope. The tank commander went berserk and caused the tank to block us from going forward. The commotion resulted in heads of the enemy appearing along [the] hedgerow to our right, going all the way back to the highway. They were Eastern troops, Mongolian in appearance. We would have taken them prisoner after opening up with machine gun fire ... but instead of surrendering, the more we fired, the more they popped up with curious looks on their faces, like who are these people? I fired about 8 boxes of ammo, until my air-cooled .30 caliber machine gun got hot enough to fire on its own. When I lowered the 37mm cannon and attached machine gun it began to fire again, just as my platoon sergeant walked by, narrowly missing him ... We got credit for killing or wounding some 60 soldiers. Our dismounted men took about 200 prisoners and 4 howitzers.'

Sgt Charles Hinds, 67th Recon Co, US 2nd Armd Div (8)

Break-out: a US tanker risks climbing outside to man the .50cal machine gun more effectively while his Sherman lays down fire on enemy troops retreating over the Marne bridges in August. (US Army)

A Sherman crew of the Canadian 4th Armd Div, which played a major part in closing the Falaise Pocket during Operation 'Totalize' in the second and third weeks of August. The German losses in the pocket — about 60,000 men and 500 armoured vehicles — crippled any German hopes of continuing the battle in France. Most Allied tank crews fixed these spare track plates and road wheels on the frontal armour to give themselves a little extra protection. (Courtesy Ed Storey)

'When we could not break through Tilly-sur-Seulles, Montgomery sent the 4th CLY right through to Villers-Bocage where we were ambushed by [501st SS Heavy Tank Battalion]. All the tanks of our leading squadron were destroyed by a couple of Tigers, and most of HQ suffered the same fate ... we fired point blank at the side of a Tiger at about 8-foot range with our Cromwell's [75mm gun] and the shell bounced off the side. Soon afterwards we were hit by the Tiger with a very different result! After we had been captured we were able to see the place where our shot had landed — it had merely smoothed the rough surface of the hull.'

Dr B. W. G. Rose, in 1944 with 4th County of London Yeomanry, British 7th Armd Div. This attack, on 13 June, was led by Capt Michael Wittmann; before being reinforced Wittmann's single Tiger crew are credited with the destruction of 21 tanks, 28 light armoured and numerous unarmoured vehicles. (9)

'We lived to see another day, but I will always remember those pathetic blackened and burnt tank crews who crawled back towards us through the burning corn. We could give them no succour, we were still engaged, and it was against standing orders to assist any disabled tank or crew during a battle. The sickening thing was, we gave them a burst of machine-gun fire, before we realised they were our own blokes creeping towards us in the corn.'

Tpr John Thorpe, 2nd Fife & Forfar Yeomanry, British 11th Armd Div (10)

British Sherman of 44th Royal Tank Regt refuelling. The constant need to replenish, check, maintain and make running repairs meant that tank crews often got even less sleep than the front line infantry. The deafening noise and nauseating fumes inside a tank in action also gave many tankers constant chronic headaches. (IWM B6192)

Preparing for battle: a British Churchill crew of 107th Regt RAC, an armoured battalion formed from the King's Own Royal Regt (Lancaster). Although the terrain of Normandy reduced most tank operations to close support of the infantry, the Churchill regiments were specifically committed to this dangerous role, since their tanks were slower and more heavily armoured than the Shermans. (IWM B7634)

'In the dark it was a matter of finding the Squadron harbour, blundering about by the light of flaming wrecks and getting mixed up with other units. It took an hour or so, and then there was the business of reorganising the Troop, taking on fuel, ammunition and rations from the Echelon trucks, reporting mechanical defects and seeing them dealt with by fitters, attending an O Group to receive orders for the next day, folding and marking maps, ensuring that a member of the crew was cooking and another arranging the bedding, sometimes fitting in a wash, or a visit to a hedge outside the harbour with a shovel and a supply of Army Form blank, which was issued on a scale two-and-a-half sheets per man per day ... It might be one, two or three in the morning, and orders were to be ready to move at dawn.

'That night after our first action, I don't think anyone slept. The petrol and ammo took three hours to reach us, the enemy were only a few hundred yards away, and everybody was shattered by the day's events. Long afterwards you thought about Cheux as just about the worst, and anything else seemed an improvement.

Lt Steel Brownlie, 2nd Fife & Forfar Yeomanry, British 11th Armd Div (11)

An M8 MGC close support howitzer passes the wreck of a fire-blackened M4 Sherman near St Lô, 25 July. The Sherman's belly plates are ripped outwards by the explosion of the stowed ammunition — the most usual cause of destruction once a solid armour-piercing shot had torn through the hull or turret. (US National Archives)

'The infantry were pinned down by Spandau fire, and there was a fair amount of mortaring, but Knocker Bell (the Squadron Leader), was prowling around on foot, with a pair of field glasses round his neck. I admired his nerve. A tank on the other side of the field brewed up. It was Sergeant Andy Roger's tank, from 1st Troop. We watched as the ammunition inside began to explode, flames and black smoke poured up. Eric Santer and Cowper baled out safely, but Sid Francis was killed, and Andy, having been carried away delirious with one leg sliced off, died shortly after ... We had lost six tanks with nothing to show for it. A message came over the air to Knocker from the CO that the Brigadier was anxious to organise a Tiger hunt. We were to withdraw immediately and take part. The last thing we wanted by then was to be involved in a Tiger hunt, but were all in favour of a withdrawal.'

Tpr Austin Baker, 4th/7th Royal Dragoon Guards, British 8th Armd Bde (12)

'We tanks are on our own, no infantry ... Don't stop for anything, charge down their anti-tank guns ... (some hope!). Climb over one railway embankment ... down to another, over the second, tanks are spread out over about 100 yards ... We are some way behind the leading ones ... when very severe armour-piercing fire comes from a coppice on our left front. Several tanks go on fire. [I fire the hull machine gun] into this coppice, while our 75mm is shooting in some AP and HE. My Browning stops, and I find the canvas bag for the empty cartridge cases is jammed full ... I pull off the bag, and feed in belt after belt, my barrel warps, and ... I try to change the barrel, but it is too hot — no matter — keep on firing, my feet are buried in a thick carpet of empties ... In front, brew-up after brew-up, some tank crews are on fire and rolling about on the ground trying to put out the flames in their clothes ... Now all the tanks in front are burning fiercely, and about 20 yards away, I see a tank boy climbing out of a turret spurting flames ... After putting one leg up to step out, he falls back inside. Ammunition explodes in the burning tanks. In the still air, huge smoke rings rise out of their turrets ... We back to the railway embankment, up over, and down the other side, into a hull-down position. ... We seem to have lost the whole of our Regiment.'

Tpr John Thorpe, 2nd Fife & Forfar Yeomanry, British 11th Armd Div (13)

(US Army)

'The smokescreen supposed to blind the enemy turned out to be a thick dense mist in the path of our advance, soon supplemented by the dust clouds created by the terrific bombing; the area was "Vision Zero". Very little could be done to keep direction, except by aiming the tank "at the sun". Speed, nothing but speed, and on we went, crashing through obstacles at 20 to 25mph ... very rough inside a tank going cross country ... We just barged ahead, some of the tanks appearing to be going on at crazy angles ... I just kept charging "at the sun", blasting everything large enough to hide a field gun and taking a terrible whipping in the turret of the bucking 32-ton monster'.

Sgt L. R. Gariépy, Fort Garry Horse, 4th Canadian Armd Div (14)

'Dave Denyer and myself went into the village of Jurques, saw the abandoned cafes, outside was an abandoned Sherman tank. The flies clustered in the open turret. Inside the tank was the commander and gunner slumped forward in their seats very dead. A small hole in the turret by an AP shell caused their death.'

Pte Eric Codling, 8th Bn, Middlesex Regt, British 43rd Inf Div (15)

'The days were long and the nights were short. A troop was in reserve one day out of four. It was usually dark — past ten o'clock when the troop reached harbour. Each individual was tired, very tired and faced with the prospect of a 4am reveille and another strenuous day ahead, his only wish was to crawl in between blankets and get some sleep. The Troop Sergeant, the busiest man of all, collected fresh rations and then split them down to vehicles. The guard for the night was detailed and several weary troopers would curse their fate. Maintenance consisted of drivers groping in the dark to check their petrol tanks, pour in one or more jerricans. For a mechanical defect the fitters would be called in, sometimes working through the night, masking their light with a tarpaulin. The Troop Leader would wait outside the CV waiting to receive his orders for the next day ... four hours of sleep was good going especially if one could take one's boots off. The month of August seemed a life-time to most people.'

Lt D. E. R. Scarr, 43rd Recce Regt, British 43rd Inf Div (16)

(Simon Pugh-Jones)

'A brewed-up tank is always a grim sight — the outside is usually a dull, dirty rust colour, and the inside is a blackened shambles. There is a queer indescribable smell. The bottom of Jonah's tank had been blown right out, and we could peer inside from underneath. There was no trace of anybody in the turret, but some stuff in the driving seat that must have been Walker. There was a body on the ground by the left-hand track. Somebody had thrown a groundsheet over it, but we lifted it off. It was probably Brigham Young, but it was impossible to recognize him — he was burnt quite black all over, and only parts of his anklets remained of his clothes. Nobody ever found any sign of Wally.'

Tpr Austin Baker, 4th/7th Royal Dragoon Guards, British 8th Armd Bde (17)

(Left) **A knocked-out M4A1 76mm Sherman blazes in a French field.** An eyewitness description from earlier in the war cannot be bettered: 'A tank that is mortally hit belches forth long searing tongues of orange flame from every hatch. As ammunition explodes in the interior, the hull is racked by violent convulsions and sparks erupt from the spout of the barrel like the fireballs of a Roman candle. Silver rivulets of molten aluminum pour from the engine like tears ... when the inferno subsides, gallons of lubricating oil in the power train and hundreds of pounds of rubber on the tracks and bogey wheels continue to burn, spewing dense clouds of black smoke over the funeral pyre.'(18)

(Simon Pugh-Jones)

'One German tanker was left lying on the road; his leg had been severed along with other wounds. No one had been available to put a tourniquet on him and he had died in a pool of blood. We captured several crew members of the disabled tanks. Two other German tanks had fled to a woods just east of us and were firing on us. I saw a lone American infantryman firing unsuccessfully at one ... with a bazooka. His attempts resulted in heavy fire directed at him, which caused him to bawl in frustration each time a round of HE hit close. He was ordered to return to the back of one of our tanks and did so. We already knew that in an open battle between a tank and a bazooka gunner, the latter would almost invariably lose the unequal contest. Any tank gunner worth his salt would know where such an infantryman would be likely to hide and would throw high explosives, machine-gun fire, or both at the unfortunate infantryman.'

Sgt Charles Hinds, 67th Recon Co, US 2nd Armd Div (19)

'On foot located brewed-up tanks — Watson and Heslewood died of wounds at Dorsets RAP. Only ash and burnt metal in Birkett's tank. Dorsets MO says other members of crew consumed by fire having been KIA. Searched ash and found remains pelvic bones. At other tank three bodies still inside — partly burned and firmly welded together. Managed with difficulty to identify Lt Campbell. Unable to remove bodies after long struggle — nasty business — sick. C Sqdn still wanting me for 2 burials; but after three unsuccessful attempts to reach them had to give up. Heavy fire each time I tried.'

Chaplain Leslie Skinner, Sherwood Rangers Yeomanry, British 8th Armd Bde; diary entry for 4 August

'Cpl. Ronan and I ... were surprised and glad to see six nice big tanks ... turn into Company Headquarters' orchard. "Always nice to have armour in support — pretty decent guns on them ... My God! German crosses on their turrets!" One tank ... knocked out a whole troop of 17-pounder anti-tank guns ...

'[It was decided that] Sgt. Hicks with his PIAT and with Cpl. Ronan's help, should start shooting up the tanks from the back. On returning [from organising three PIAT teams I watched] Maj. Fry and Ptes. Jeffries and Parrish being chased around the orchard. [The tanks] knocked out the two 6-pounder guns in D Company area, wounding most of the crew. Battalion Headquarters was ... a nice hull-down shoot at about 50 yards range. Our 6-pounders replied despite [being] under direct fire. Lt Col Atherton was killed [trying] to keep one gun firing.

'Four PIATs were hitting the tanks ... one fled, hit three times ... Sgt. Hicks knocked out another ... and two more went round the corner and Capt. Blackwell of C Company ... knocked one out and the other turned over in its excitement to escape.'

Capt H.Jobson, 5th Bn, Duke of Cornwall's Light Infantry, British 43rd Inf Div (21)

'Our PIAT was spring-loaded. It had to be cocked before firing the first round and the easiest way to cock it was standing upright with both feet fixed firmly on the shoulder piece. The spring's recoil, so it was said, would recock the weapon. If the PIAT misfired, it had to be recocked again. Imagine it! Standing up in view of the enemy to pull on a strong spring. The shell it fired was shaped like a turnip. It was fitted into a cutout section on the top side of the PIAT. The sights were primitive and the range was short: effectively, about 50 yards. When the turnip flew through the air it had to strike its target squarely ... I must admit that when a PIAT grenade did explode a lot of damage was caused. I do not think it could penetrate the front armour of a Tiger tank, but it could smash through the side and rear armour ... The number of Panzers which were knocked out were very, very few when one considers how many PIATs were in use.'

**Raymond Rolls, British
7th Armd Div (22)**

(US National Archives)

Early August 1944: a US infantry bazooka team in action in the hedgerows. Shoulder-fired anti-tank weapons could penetrate the weaker side and rear armour of the tanks, but only from very close range — perhaps 50 yards. It took a brave and lucky soldier to knock out several tanks, and on both sides such men were often decorated for gallantry. Tank machine gunners and their accompanying infantry would normally lay down a storm of suppressive fire on any nearby cover which might hide a tank-killer team - visibility from inside a tank was too bad for crews to try to spot individual targets of this kind.

'*C Company advanced up Hill 112 and despite mortar, shelling and small arms gained the top astride the Caen-Esquay road, but were pinned down by dug-in Tigers and machine guns firing from Esquay. CSM Smith in a Bren gun carrier bringing up ammo saw a tank shooting its way along the road towards the prostrate company, grabbed a PIAT, ran through the cornfield, fired it from the hip and knocked out the tank, for which he received a merited MM [Military Medal].*'
Capt John McMath, 5th Bn, Wiltshire Regt, British 43rd Inf Div (23)

(Below) PIAT (Projector, Infantry, Anti-Tank) crew from the British 51st Highland Division; each platoon had one of these weapons. Firing was initiated by a spring-loaded spigot striking the percussion cap of the rocket-propelled bomb. The discharge was supposed to cock the very strong spring for the next shot, but sometimes failed; it took a man's whole body strength to cock it manually, pushing down on the butt with the feet and arching the back — a contortion hard to perform safely in combat. (IWM B8913)

(Tony Holmes)

Civilians

'Lt John Eisenhower, the supreme commander's son, newly graduated from West Point and on a tour of the front, wrote after visiting the British sector: "The attitude of the French was sobering indeed. Instead of bursting with enthusiasm they seemed not only indifferent but sullen. There was considerable cause for wondering whether these people wished to be liberated."

And Chief of the British General Staff General Sir Alan Brooke noted with displeasure, "The French population did not seem in any way pleased to see us arrive as a victorious army to liberate France. They had been quite content as they were, and we were bringing war and desolation to their country."' (1)

(Photos US National Archives)

'St Honorine-la-Chardonne was the first inhabited village we had liberated, the population was about four thousand. As the first troop entered the village, the church bells began ringing and men, women and children ran into the streets to greet us. The pavements were lined with the inhabitants offering us buckets and buckets of cider, calvados and abundant fruit. The German troops had left two hours before. A French liaison officer arrived to take charge of the administration. The village turned into a rest area for us. We had cinema shows and ENSA shows for entertainment.'

**L/Cpl Ron Garner, 5th Bn,
Wiltshire Regt, British 43rd Inf Div (2)**

The British Front

(Tony Holmes)

(Below) A British corporal leads his infantry section into a granite-built Normandy village, 26 June. Most men carry large picks and shovels thrust under their packs — the issue entrenching tool was too small to get Tommies underground fast enough when they expected artillery and mortar fire. (IWM B5968)

'[The brigadier] gave us a pep talk before we sailed for Normandy. It went like this. "We are going over the water tomorrow. Some of you will be blown to pieces but that doesn't matter. But I want you to understand that if anyone deserts, he will be court-martialled and he will be shot" — very comforting.'

Stan Procter, 1st Bn, Worcestershire Regt, British 43rd Inf Div (1)

(Right) Operation 'Epsom', 26 June: men of **B Company, 6th Bn, Royal Scots Fusiliers from 15th Scottish Div** prepare to attack the village of St Mauvieu. It will be taken — but B Company will suffer 50 per cent casualties. At full strength the infantry section, led by a Sten-armed corporal, had a three-man Bren gun team and six other riflemen; three sections and a small headquarters group made up a platoon. In periods of prolonged combat platoons often had to operate at half strength or less. (IWM B5959)

'The short drive through the Normandy countryside similar to Kent, evidence of invasion near the road. Knocked-out tanks and other vehicles, abandoned guns and ammo littered the road and fields. Roadside graves both Allied and German with makeshift mark of rifle stuck in the ground and steel helmet placed on top indicated the bridgehead had been dearly paid for. For us a sobering thought. Our carriers were dispersed in a large meadow under large trees growing in the thick wide hedgerows. Our first sight of the infamous "bocage" in which we were to suffer badly in the near future.'
Pte Eric Codling, 8th Bn, Middlesex Regt, British 43rd Inf Div (2)

'18 Platoon was an example of how the battalion had suffered — Lt Pinkham and Sgt Popham had both been wounded and evacuated, also Cpl Maslin. Although I could see strangers in the platoon, which meant reinforcements had been received, we were sadly only at half strength. Slit trenches had been scraped out of the bare, open slope and I joined a young soldier barely 19 years old, who occupied a slit on his own. He was pleased to have company. Snipers were very active — as were the "Moaning Minnies", which put the fear of God into us. They were multiple-firing mortars that could discharge a cluster of bombs at one firing, and whilst in trajectory emitted a weird wailing noise ... There was no roaming around our platoon or company area during daylight; once in our slit trenches we stayed put, venturing out only when absolutely essential.'
Cpl Douglas Proctor, 4th Bn, Somerset Light Infantry, British 43rd Inf Div (3)

Operation 'Epsom', 26 June: infantry of **15th Scottish Div** advance through the *bocage* supported by a Churchill tank — which is forced to expose its thinner underside armour to enemy fire as it crawls over the bank. (IWM B6124)

'The bocage in which the 50th Division was now fighting was entirely different from anything they had encountered before. There are many woods and orchards. It is granite country, and over the centuries the peasants had built the outcropping chunks of granite into the fences and hedges. The undergrowth has grown up through the rocks, so that every hedge is a natural fortified obstacle. The fields are small, and the roads are often sunk below the level of the fields. The houses and farms are built of granite, and each is a ready-made fortress.'

Pte Tom Tateson, 7th Bn, Green Howards, British 50th Inf Div (5)

'The whole of this period 26 29 June was one of the most trying periods I went through. We were shelled pretty consistently the whole time we were there and night was absolute hell. None of us could have had more than one hour's sleep in twenty-four and the Boche was expected to make his big effort at any moment to push us back into the sea.'

Maj Anthony Jeans, 4th Bn, Wiltshire Regt, British 43rd Inf Div (6)

'I can see again the earth banks, the green hedgerows, the white dust of Normandy, and I can feel again the hush and quiet, the grim and threatening quiet, that broods over a front-line position. The men, their faces strained, speak in low, tired voices, almost fearful of breaking a spell ...

'As soon as darkness fell we could hear the crackle of a Spandau or the burrp-burrp of a machine-pistol as the Boche once again began his night's work. During the day the crash of a sniper's rifle or the sudden mounting crescendo of mortar bombs, preceded by the unearthly groan of the rocket projector, causing dozing men to stare at each other and bolt to their slit trenches, holding themselves rigid while the smash of bombs tore through the air.'

Maj Cooke, 8th Bn, Royal Scots, British 15th Scottish Div (4)

(Martin Brayley0)

(Tony Holmes)

'We hit the earth with one thud where we had stood. I could feel the exact spot in the small of my defenceless back (I wish to God we had packs on ... not because they're any use but it feels better) where the pointd nose of the shell would pierce skin and gristle and bone and explode the charge that would make me feel as if I had a splitting headache all over for a fiftieth of a second before I was spread minutely over the earth and hung up in trees. I held my breath and tried to press deeper into the earth and tensed every muscle as though by sheer willpower I could ... cheat death ... (Oh God have mercy upon me, please, please dear God, don't let me die!)'

Pte S. Bagnall, 5th Bn, East Lancashire Regt, British 197 Inf Bde
(7)

'[I was] shaken, using a thick hedgerow as a latrine, to discover that the mound of earth which [I] squatted beside had a pair of jack boots protruding from the far end. Our Somerset LI neighbours captured a young lad from the Hitler Youth SS Div. We were amazed at his arrogance as he approached his captors, combing his blond locks; only minutes before he had been sniping at them from trees until his ammo ran out.'

Pte Eric Codling, 8th Bn, Middlesex Regt, British 43rd Inf Div
(8)

(Tony Holmes)

'While moving up ... the company carrier was blown up killing four men ... We were now in range of enemy mortars ... and casualties were becoming more frequent. I was not feeling very brave now. One of my mates said he couldn't stop his knees from knocking ... I was in good company. Our support was marvellous. The Artillery was pounding the enemy then lifting up 100 yards every four minutes. Jerry was not idle. Air bursts were exploding overhead. We hated them. We came into a field next to the first buildings of Mouen; several Scottish soldiers were lying dead across the field. When about 40 yards from the building, a machine gun opened up from an upstairs window. My reaction was instant. I whipped up my [Bren] gun and fired a burst across the window. Whether I hit anyone or not, I did not know nor did I care. The attack was a great success. To survive was purely a matter of luck.'

Pte Albert Kings, 1st Bn, Worcestershire Regt, British 43rd Inf Div (9)

'The country between Cheux and the Odon is very close, a lot of orchards, small fields ... it was necessary for the rifle companies to advance on compass bearings. After crossing the Caen/Villers-Bocage railway we came under a particularly nasty concentration of artillery fire. L/Cpl. Stanley Burfield, my company clerk was killed beside me. I was slightly wounded ... We finally got down into the valley of the Odon river named initially by the soldiers "Happy Valley", then for obvious reasons, "Death Valley". The Somerset and Wiltshire salient was two miles deep and a mile across. The Germans were on three sides of us and could fire on us with a variety of mortars, artillery and that unpleasant weapon the Moaning Minnie or Nebelwerfer.'

Capt John Majendie, 4th Bn, Somerset Light Infantry, British 43rd Inf Div (10)

'For four days and nights there was no let up. I was surprised with all the firing, the guns being so hot did not blow up. [We ran out of ammunition and] ... for the first time the guns were quiet, a SOS was sent out for supplies. Two other regiments came to our aid and immediately four counter attacks were broken up ... Although I did not seem to be frightened with the guns firing at us, the bombs, the machine guns, mortars, etc I did fear the snipers hidden in the trees. You knew when you heard the crack of a solitary rifle that one of your mates was now dead. I saw several snipers hanging in the trees.'

Gnr Philip Guppy, British 94th Field Regt, RA (11)

(Martin Brayley/0

'... very brave young Germans who strapped themselves into trees. When they were spotted and fired on, they were killed or wounded. There was no way to come down, they merely hung in the trees.'

Capt John Majendie, 4th Bn, Somerset Light Infantry, British 43rd Inf Div (12)

'The Battalion left Colleville at midnight: there was no moon and it was very dark. All was quiet, except for shells from both sides that swished overhead ... But what had started off as a pleasant night time stroll deteriorated into a nightmare as the Cornish men reached the railway track. In places the rails had been torn up and jagged fingers of twisted steel bit into unwary ankles; shell holes pitted the track, and bodies littering the banks looked like grotesque, lurking enemy.

'Broken telegraph poles had fallen across the rails. But worst of all was the wire. It was everywhere — telegraph wire, railway wire, signal cable, all tossed up on the track like tangled knitting wool. And in the darkness men stumbled, sweated, tripped, and cursed their way forward, now more concerned with the obstacles in their path than with the sudden flash and burst of falling mortar bombs or the tracer flying in thin pencil lines above.'

Capt Bill Gorman, 5th Bn, Duke of Cornwall's Light Infantry, British 43rd Inf Div (13)

'The snipers, of course, are a law unto themselves. They submit to the fatherly will of CSM Davidson, MM; but apart from that they go their own ways regardless of what the rest of the Battalion does, what Standing Orders say, or what three brigades, the Divisional Artillery, and the machine-gunners think they are doing. You can easily spot them when the Battalion is settling down for the night. In quite the most comfortable corner, but at the same time at a discreet distance from the Regimental Sergeant Major's habitation, you will see a bundle of shapeless figures in a variety of dress gathered like tinkers round a blazing fire which has clearly been made up regardless either of black-out or of petrol scarcity. A savoury sizzling smell rises from the centre of the group, and a cloud of white feathers eddies in the evening breeze. In the background a murder is being committed. The shrieks of the victim die away in an ominous gurgling, and a red-headed figure smoking a pipe appears out of the gloom carrying the corpse — a fat young porker. To call this independent band a problem is understating it. They are a menace to all order-loving sergeant-majors whenever we are out of the line. Luckily they are even more of a menace to the enemy at anything under four hundred yards when we are in contact.'

Maj Richard Fleming, 5th Bn, Seaforth Highlanders,

(IWM B6851)

In a row of hastily-dug slit trenches along the edge of a Normandy field, one man keeps watch while his mate tries to snatch some sleep. Lack of sleep, and the carelessness which it caused, is mentioned by many veterans. **(IWM B6851, B7441)**

'We were suddenly marched hotfoot to rejoin the battalion which was suffering heavy casualties. We were rushed up the slope of Hill 112, directed towards Bn HQ, on the other side of a hedge. Before crossing the hedge I was a signal corporal. On landing in the trench I was acting Signal Sergeant. On contacting the few signallers remaining I found our casualties were appalling. Fifteen men were left of one [rifle] company. We were shelled unmercifully. Casualties mounted. The cries "stretcher-bearers, stretcher-bearers" were piteous and almost continuous.'

Sgt Leo Davis, 4th Bn, Wiltshire Regt, British 43rd Inf Div (15)

'It had seemed so easy all these weeks since D-Day to make ourselves comfortable below ground, adding one refinement to another as we moved from place to place and our skill grew. The firm clay of Normandy made good digging, and we soon learned to make ourselves snug. Although the basic model was only a pit six feet long by two-and-a-half wide by four or five feet deep with a sheet of corrugated iron and a heap of earth on top, there were many things a man could do to improve it. There were doovers lined with parachute silk, doovers with electric light, mosquito-proof doovers with face-veils over the entrances. Doors were lifted from their hinges and used to strengthen roofs (though some preferred earth-filled wardrobes), and few houses had a shutter left five minutes after the Battalion moved into an area. Then the weather broke.

'The thunderstorm broke upon us on the afternoon of July 20, and by evening the whole place was a shambles. Nothing that human ingenuity could devise would keep the tide at bay. We baled. We made roofs with gas-capes. We piled compo boxes into the mud and lay on them, only to be wakened as the water lapped over the top. By morning our trenches had three feet of water in them and we were driven into the open, soaking and without hope, with the rain falling.'

Capt Alastair Borthwick, 5th Bn, Seaforth Highlanders, British 51st Highland Div (16)

(IWM B7441)

(Tony Holmes)

'From the 9th until the 16th July our routine was the same. During the night, two sentries per section were on watch, with the others on immediate call. At 0430 hours we stood-to, peering miserably from our trenches into the gloomy hedgerows, feeling too bleary and cold to care whether the Germans appeared or not. At some time between 0530 and 0600, depending on visibility, we went back to whatever we happened to be calling our bed, wrapped the dew-damp blankets around us, and slept until 0900 hours. Then the petrol fires were started and the compo rations were cooked for breakfast. In theory, one made good during the rest of the morning the sleep lost during sentry-go at night, but I never met anyone who claimed to have been able to do so. There was always some job to do, or some conference to attend, or a shell to be dodged; and then it was evening again, with the serenade going full blast. If it had rained it would have been a loathsome existence; as it was, the sun shone and life was tolerable ...

[The mosquitoes], far bigger and more inquisitive than any we had encountered in Africa ... caused more discomfort and loss of sleep in the Orne bridgehead than ever shelling did.'

Capt Alastair Borthwick, 5th Bn, Seaforth Highlanders, British 51st Highland Div (17)

(Tony Holmes)

(IWM B5951)

'In the first attack [on Etterville] early in the morning it seems that the enemy let the leading platoon of D Coy under Lt. J. Hayes go past and then opened up with their MG — he and almost all his platoon were killed. In the second attack, Maltot on our left was to have been taken by 7 Hants but the attack failed so 4 Dorsets were ordered to attack. They had a very bad time ... Our flank was exposed owing to the failure to take Maltot and Hill 112 was still in enemy hands ... Enemy armour together with infantry tried to dislodge us but as always our supporting gunner 112 Field Regt gave us magnificent support and we stayed put.'

(Capt Maurice Edwards, 5th Bn, Dorsetshire Regt, British 43rd Inf Div (18)

'I was the leading platoon commander in B Coy. We advanced with our Maori Totem pole shouting the Maori war cry. The totem was a 6ft holly stick with a brass jug that we had pinched from a local pub in Dorset and the whole platoon had scratched their names on it. On top ... was the skull of a cow ...

'As soon as we dug in on the northern outskirts [of Etterville] we stuck our Platoon Totem in the ground Many Tiger tanks were swanning around and one silly one blew our Totem to pieces with a shell. Immediately my anti-tank chap stood and knocked out the tank with his ... [PIAT] which was not supposed to do any damage to a Tiger tank. We made short work of the tank and its crew. We had many casualties.'

Capt R. F. Hall, 4th Bn, Dorsetshire Regt, British 43rd Inf Div (19)

'We had no difficulty in repulsing the infantry, the fire discipline being first class and both companies giving the Boche absolute hell. It was grand to hear the section commanders shouting out their orders: "Hold your fire, chaps, until you can see the buggers' eyes." It did fearful execution ... The CO — Col. James — was magnificent. He set an outstanding example to everyone by his personal courage ... we were still rather green, but for him, I don't know what might have happened.'

Maj Bob Roberts, 5th Bn, Duke of Cornwall's Light Infantry, British 43rd Inf Div (20)

'When [Col. James] was killed alongside me it was my duty as one of the signallers at the time to report to rear HQ, that as far as I could see there were no officers or senior NCOs left unwounded to command the battalion. Never was anyone more welcome then ... when Maj. John Fry, having handed over command of D Company, made his way through the wood to the command post to take over the Bn. He rallied the survivors and organised their defensive fire to best effect. It became

(Tony Holmes)

obvious that very soon there would be nothing left of us, if the remnant of the Bn was not soon withdrawn.'

Pte Jack Foster, 5th Bn, Duke of Cornwall's Light Infantry, British 43rd Inf Div (21)

'Lippy [Lt Col C. G. Lipscomb, OC 4th Somersets] was outstanding in many difficult situations and none more so than when the remnants of 5 DCLI after a terrible time in Cornwall Wood on Hill 112, came back into our positions. He rallied them and sensing a crisis drew his pistol and shouted "I'll shoot the first Somerset who goes back". And an honest private soldier in my company told me, years later, "When I saw the DCLI coming I put on my small pack and if they'd gone I was going with them" ...

'[Later the 5th DCLI] reformed and very gallantly went back into Cornwall Wood and Clifford Perks, our A/Tank Platoon Commander, went back with them to give advice on their very diminished anti-tank protection. Again later in the afternoon it was quite impossible for them. They were about down to Company strength — their casualties were increasing all the time and they again retired back to our battalion position and dug in to the left of my company.'

Capt John Majendie, 4th Bn, Somerset Light Infantry, British 43rd Inf Div (22)

'[Lt Donald Pope] decided to go in with the bayonet under cover of his Brens and 2-in mortar and shouting at his chaps to follow he ran forward firing his Sten from the hip. He had not gone far across this 50 yards of hell before he was hit

again. He fell, but scrambled up and ran on, only to be hit again, this time in the other leg. He decided that it was too big a job for him as only two men had followed him so he started to come back but was hit a fourth time. This time he went down for the count in the middle of No Man's Land.'

Maj Anthony Jeans, 4th Bn, Wiltshire Regt, British 43rd Inf Div (23)

'The Battalion formed up with two companies up and two in reserve. The Companies entered [Maltot] village supported by tanks protecting the flanks, only to be met with terrific opposition. Tanks were knocked out from all directions. Tigers were concealed in orchards, and machine-guns fired from all angles. Neither we nor the Hampshires stood an earthly chance of securing the village. Most of our tracked vehicles were knocked out by 88s. Our anti-tank gunners did not have time to place their guns in position ... At about 19.00 hours, orders were given to withdraw to the original start line, dig in and hold. Remnants of the companies came back, but A Company complete had been killed, wounded or captured.'

Sgt Wally Caines, 4th Bn, Dorsetshire Regt, British 43rd Inf Div (24)

'Maltot proved to be a dreadful spectacle, the streets and fields were still strewn with the dead [Dorsets and Hampshires killed on 10 July] ... The houses were shattered, roads cratered and full of debris; everywhere the sickly smell of death and destruction hung heavily upon the ruins. Enemy Tiger tanks overlooking the village were still dropping shells with deadly accuracy on our positions. Direct hits on two

(cont. overleaf)

Men of 6th Royal Scots Fusiliers during street-fighting in St Mauvieu, 26 June. (IWM B5963)

slit trenches killed two company commanders ... A squadron of tanks came up to reinforce the position. They met disaster in a few seconds, seven [Churchills] ... were set on fire from direct hits ... Eventually RAF Typhoons rocketed three Tigers. But thirty-six hours after the Bn first reached the village, hungry, bomb-happy German soldiers emerged from various hiding places — trenches, cellars, cupboards, stables. Eventually the tally came to over 400 from a well-armed fresh enemy division.'
Capt John McMath, 5th Bn, Wiltshire Regt, British 43rd Inf Div (25)

'One German soldier ran towards us from the left flank. His hands were raised as if surrendering but I could see he was still armed with a few stick grenades that were in his belt. His arm dropped and grasped a grenade; without the slightest hesitation or compunction, I shot him.'
Cpl Douglas Proctor, 4th Bn, Somerset Light Infantry, British 43rd Inf Div (26)

(Martin Brayley)

(Right & below) On 9/10 July the Canadian infantry finally drove the SS 'Hitlerjugend' Div out of Caen and the surrounding villages. (Canadian National Archives PA131398/ Ken Bell; & PA115028/H.Aikman)

'In the dark on the road two enemy halftracks drove right into our midst firing their machine guns like mad ... Most of us were scurrying around looking for non-existent cover in the dark. Maj. Whitehead took immediate action. He snatched the loaded PIAT gun out of my hands, thrust his rifle at me. He then fired one shot at the first halftrack which exploded and burst into flame. He then took up his rifle and fired at a German. The man fell back into the flames with his arms outspread. No.10 Platoon had not got their PIAT ready to fire so the second halftrack escaped.'

Pte Len Stokes, 7th Bn, Somerset Light Infantry, British 43rd Inf Div (27)

'Before us stretched three glorious carefree days of rest. The sheer bliss of a bath, the luxury of clean underwear. Parties of all ranks went to Bayeaux. With two of my officers we dined with a French family there. There were ENSA and cinema shows. A small party of nurses visited the battalion and were entertained in the HQ mess. The war could have been a million miles away.'

Lt Col George Taylor, 5th Bn, Duke of Cornwall's Light Infantry, British 43rd Inf Div (28)

'24 July. All quiet on the western front and the sun is shining ... poor old Johnny Hiscocks got his eyes damaged by the blast of a shell from a Tiger tank, Paul Gornich, the little major with glasses, went mad, John Tilley just got a Blighty in the shoulder. I did not lose too many men compared to some.

26 July. Bn coming out of line to refit after five weeks on the go, the whole time. The French civilians do not seem very interested either way. Poor devils, I expect they are tired of being occupied.

28 July. I have been able to buy over 300 cigarettes, two bottles of Scotch, one of gin, so life looks brighter ... I spent an hour in the [Bayeaux] cathedral with my old CO — Tim Wood — glorious building reminiscent of Notre Dame. I have come back from a Communion Service. I feel better for it, does me a lot of good.'

Lt Col Gerald Tilley, 5th Bn, Dorsetshire Regt, British 43rd Inf Div, in a letter to his wife (29)

'3 August. 'O' group to attack Ondefontaine 2½ miles ahead. 1330 hrs attack commenced. Forward troop left their trenches only to meet stiff enemy resistance. They were cut down like flies — every man pinned to the ground as all round Spandaus fired murderously. There was no hope of advancing. Our artillery plastered the Jerries. The attack kept up for about an hour then it was decided to withdraw to the original position. Our casualties were very heavy ... and many men still laid wounded amongst the dead in the cornfield. Some managed to crawl back to safety, others laid up until dark whilst a few remained to die of their wounds and where they fell.'

Sgt Wally Caines, 4th Bn, Dorsetshire Regt, British 43rd Inf Div (30)

'4 August. An uncomfortable feeling as we rode along closely packed on top of the Sherman tanks of B Sqn 13/18th Hussars and our already overloaded wheeled and tracked vehicles ... countryside resembled Devon, steep and wooded hills, lanes with high banks, large undulating cornfields.

'5 August. At Ecures ... the bridge blown and both banks mined. On the way to St Jean le Blanc up the steep slopes it was slow, costly bitter work by C Company; eight hours of desperate fighting under a burning sun. Our [artillery Forward Observation Officer] Capt. J. Fletcher was tireless, invaluable. L/Cpl. Jenkins (A Coy) commanded a platoon reduced to seven men, and for his daring later received the MM ... That night C Coy dug in, hungry and exhausted with the sad task of burying their dead ... Capt. Fletcher fed every man in the Company with biscuits, bully beef and water from his carrier. A bitter and largely fruitless day's fighting in difficult country under the hot sun ... We lost twenty-two killed and thirty-nine wounded.'

Maj A. D. Parsons, 4th Bn, Wiltshire Regt, British 43rd Inf Div (31)

'The approach march to our forming up place had been a nightmare of swirling abrasive dust, shelling and the stench of exhaust fumes from our tanks that transported us forward ... The ground before us descended to a small stream at the foot of Mt Pinçon then rose steeply through typical bocage fields with thick hedgerows to a thickly wooded area. The top of the hill was open and crowned with gorse. The forward platoon of B Coy had barely crossed the stream when concentrated Spandau fire came from the front and from both flanks. There must have been about twelve machine guns firing at one time. This devastating firepower stopped the Bn dead in its tracks. There was no way forward or around it and no way to retire.'

Lt Sydney Jary, 4th Bn, Somerset Light Infantry, British 43rd Inf Div (32)

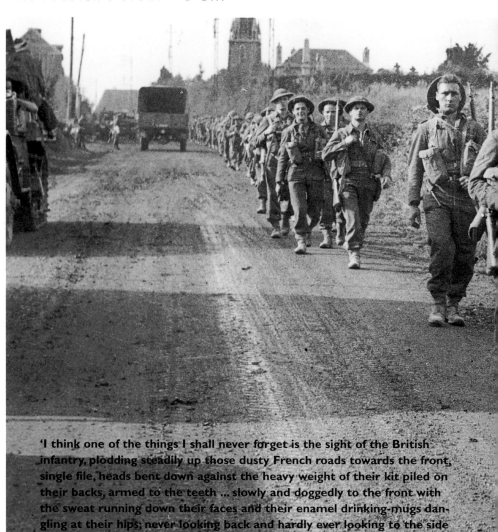

'I think one of the things I shall never forget is the sight of the British infantry, plodding steadily up those dusty French roads towards the front, single file, heads bent down against the heavy weight of their kit piled on their backs, armed to the teeth ... slowly and doggedly to the front with the sweat running down their faces and their enamel drinking-mugs dangling at their hips; never looking back and hardly ever looking to the side — just straight in front ... while the jeeps and the lorries and the tanks and all the other traffic went crowding by, smothering them in great billows and clouds of dust which they never even deigned to notice. That was a sight that somehow caught at your heart'. (Wg Cdr L.Nickolls, RAF) (39) (IWM B8560)

'As dusk fell a new plan was drawn up. The night air was chilly and misty and a smokescreen was laid across the entire valley at the foot of the mountains ... The new plan was for each company to infiltrate the enemy positions advancing stealthily in single file. The night and darkness was our ally ... the German soldier didn't relish night fighting. It seems incredible that a battalion of infantry having once been stopped for dead, could rise up like wraiths from the mist and slowly but inexorably advance to the top of the hill. Not one shot was fired against us. We slipped by their positions without being noticed ... On the summit we were cold, wet and thoroughly miserable being in shirt-sleeve order. At about 7a.m. a very welcome meal reached us.'

Cpl Douglas Proctor, 4th Bn, Somerset Light Infantry, British 43rd Inf Div (33)

'We dug furiously to make a suitable trench. Every few minutes a German MG would fire into the area, make us duck. After two feet down we struck water. Once a salvo of mortars landed. I dived into a sewer to find three other men in occupation — one reading his pocket Bible. ... We had well over a hundred prisoners. A few of them were put to work digging graves for our men who had fallen. They thought it was for themselves ... We had a total of sixty-six men left from all the four rifle companies put together.'

L/Cpl Ron Garner, 5th Bn, Wiltshire Regt, British 43rd Inf Div (34)

'We followed the line of a hedge until we found A Coy dug in there. About twenty-five men were resting in their slit trenches, asked them if they were part of A Coy. I still remember the look in the fellow's eyes as he answered "We are ****ing A Company."'

Pte J. V. Webb, 4th Bn, Wiltshire Regt, British 43rd Inf Div (35)

'During the afternoon our signals intercepted a message from Monty saying "the end was in sight". Naturally we could not see this but later realised this was the beginning of the Falaise pocket. News came through that 3,000 enemy vehicles had been shot up during the day by the RAF ... On the 14th the Bn moved to La Rue in a valley near Condé. Hundreds of French refugees came to greet us and beg for food. They were a pitiful sight and we couldn't very well refuse: out came our tins of sardines and corned beef. What they wanted most of all was bread. They were given army dog biscuits and seemed to enjoy them quite a lot.'

L/Cpl Ron Garner, 5th Bn, Wiltshire Regt, British 43rd Inf Div (36)

'We fired 600 rounds per gun into the Falaise pocket. The observation and reconnaissance vehicles returning to our lines were washed down with disinfectant to remove human and animal debris from them. Dead friend and foe alike — for there were many French civilians trapped in the area — lay in heaps, their bodies mixed together with horses and domestic animals, filling the sunken lanes where they had sought shelter. So intense was the carnage of man and beast, that all the dead animals could not be buried and later these were bulldozed into heaps and set on fire with petrol.'

Sgt Sam Beard, British 179th Field Regt Royal Artillery (37) .

'Near Falaise, massed slaughter had taken place by Typhoon fighter bombers. The recce party passed through this area. We travelled one road and actually our vehicle travelled over the top of many crushed German dead bodies ... how that lot looked and stank, dead bodies were running over with maggots and flies — it was indeed a ghastly sight seeing these dead Nazis bursting in the blistering heat of the day. The road was about 1½ miles long. Never before had I seen or smelt anything like it.'

Sgt Wally Caines, 4th Bn, Dorsetshire Regt, British 43rd Inf Div (38)

Obergrenadier Gerhard Zurborg of SS Pz-Gren Regt 26 was four days short of his 19th birthday when he was killed in Normandy on 27 June. His unit of the 'Hitlerjugend' Div apparently held the ground long enough to give him a proper marker; now they have gone, and British Sherman tanks pass by on their way east, across France towards the Low Countries and Germany. (IWM B6221)

Casualties

During the fighting in Normandy between 6 June and 30 August 1944 it is estimated that approximately 124,000 American soldiers were killed, wounded or taken prisoner. The British total was around 64,000, the Canadian some 18,000, the Polish around 2,000 — making an Allied total of about 208,000 casualties. German losses in killed, wounded and captured for the same period are estimated at about 400,000 men.

Although casualty rates among the Allied armies as a whole were much lower than in 1914-18, losses within individual combat units were often extremely high — comparable to those of World War I. For instance, between 6 and 30 June 1944 the three-battalion US 12th Inf Regt, 4th Inf Div, lost 76 per cent of its officers and 63 per cent of its enlisted men. The US 2nd Inf Div suffered 1,200 casualties, most of them in its nine infantry battalions, over the three days of its first attempt to take Hill 192 near St Lô. In the seven weeks from D-Day to 31 July the average losses in the rifle companies of the US 1st, 4th, 9th and 29th Inf Divs were 68.7 per cent of the officers and 59.6 per cent of the enlisted men. These are average figures; some divisions fared worse. The 90th Inf Div lost the equivalent of 100 per cent of its strength in six weeks, with some rifle companies recording 400 per cent casualties — i.e. the

equivalent of the whole company being wiped out completely and replaced, four times. The three month Normandy campaign cost the British 3rd Inf Div 7,100 casualties — i.e. about 115 per cent of its infantry strength — including 904 killed outright; and one battalion of the 51st (Highland) Div lost 44 officers, or 133 per cent of establishment.

However, huge advances had been made in medical science since World War I. By 1944 penicillin was widely available to the Allied armies, and combated local wound sepsis; it is estimated that it saved 12 to 15 per cent of cases which would otherwise have been fatal. Sulphonamides ('sulfa' tablets and powder, carried by every GI) combated systemic septicaemia. Finally, the ability to store whole blood and plasma for transfusion greatly increased survival rates.

In 1944 survival rates — among those wounded who lived long enough to reach treatment by medical officers — were remarkably high; and although an individual's fate was entirely dependent on the local tactical situation, in NW Europe the majority of the wounded were evacuated from the battlefield fast enough to receive expert care. Among those who reached such help, the survival rate among those who suffered abdominal wounds was between 70 and 75 per cent; the equivalent figures for chest wounds and traumatic amputations were about 94 per cent and 80 per cent respectively, and even head wounds had a better than 50 per cent chance of survival (though of immediately fatal wounds, 47 per cent were to the head). We repeat, however, that these figures applied only to those who lived long enough to receive treatment.

The weapons of 20th century warfare inflicted wounds ranging all the way from

a trivial nick by a tiny shrapnel fragment, or a single clean bullet hole (though even a rifle bullet, tumbling on contact, could cause massive destruction of tissue), to ghastly dismemberment or, in the case of direct hits by heavy shells and bombs, almost total destruction. As a rough rule, about 25-30 per cent of casualties were gunshot wounds (of whom those hit by machine-gun fire were nearly twice as likely to die immediately as those hit by rifle bullets). Nearly all the rest were caused by artillery and mortar fire.

In a surprising number of accounts the reaction of wounded men is described as muted and restrained, as traumatic shock provided a natural anaesthetic. In cases of gross burning, dismemberment or disembowelment some men screamed for a merciful bullet, others lost their minds. There is no purpose in repetitive quotation of horrors. The descriptions which follow would seem to cover enough of the range of soldiers' experiences to paint a sufficiently vivid picture. (1)

**(Right) Between 7 and 10 per cent of Allied casualties were caused by the large numbers of landmines sown by the Wehrmacht when fighting on the defensive. Small 'shoe mines' were just large enough to blow off a man's foot — an economical way of tying up several other men to care for and evacuate him. The more lethal S-mine (which GIs called 'Bouncing Betty') had a propellant charge which blew it about 4 feet in the air before the main charge detonated, sending shrapnel scything in all directions. It needed a ground pressure of only 7lbs to set it off.
(US National Archives)**

**Blood stockpiled by the US Army Medical Corps before Operation 'Cobra', 25 July. During the whole North-West Europe campaign the US Army used more than 48,000 gallons of whole blood and plasma. Comparable British figures suggest that the average casualty received a transfusion of about 4 pints.
(US National Archives)**

(Tony Holmes)

(Simon Pugh-Jones)

(Below) 14 June: a major of the 6th Bn, Durham Light Infantry from British 50th Div enjoys a smoke, and apparently the slight euphoria of a lightly wounded man after treatment, painkillers, and the first steps of his evacuation to the rear areas. He has earned it; his ribbons show the award of a Military Cross in Africa.
(IWM B5529)

'[He] was in such agony that after a moment or two he had fainted, the [rifle] bullet having hit him in the forearm and broken the bone. He is the only man whom I have ever seen in pain from a wound, the shock being normally so great that nothing much is felt for some hours.'

Lt Col Martin Lindsay, 1st Bn, Gordon Highlanders, British 51st Highland Div (4)

'A black fog was swirling, my whole body felt numb, I was all sort of peculiar, my right leg appeared to be twisted in near my left shoulder, my boot blown off ... I suddenly thought of fire and screamed out to [the corporal] to get me out, that I couldn't move. I was pulled from the cab and laid on a stretcher alongside about ten others, wounded by the mine which I had run over. My officer came back and wished me luck and put packets of cigarettes under my blanket. I lay there about an hour ...

'A medical officer, his own arm in a sling, examined my foot and put my field dressing on [it] ... and then a rifle was bandaged to my leg as a splint. I was moved into the garden of a house. A wounded German was sitting on the ground and I threw him a cigarette ... I arrived back in England [on] 8th June, and my right leg was amputated in Haslar Hospital.'

Dvr G. S. Squires, 172 Co RASC, British 3rd Inf Div (5)

'C Company was to spearhead the diamond formation for the attack. My company commander ... and I agreed we should keep as close behind our artillery barrage as possible — perhaps risking casualties from our own guns. We would descend upon the enemy stunned by the weight of our artillery shells. This tactic paid off handsomely. The only casualty was ME! An almighty crash about 20 yards to my left and I felt a great smack on my left arm, buttock and shoulder. A big wham. And then no pain. The adrenalin was flowing and we stormed on.'

Lt Peter Hall, 1st Bn, Worcestershire Regt, British 43rd Inf Div (2)

'The medics came over ... the second asked me how badly I was hit. I told him I didn't know I was hit. The medic removed my gas mask, which was worn chest-high for buoyancy, and showed me a hole through it and then he showed me a hole in my shirt. He cut away my shirt and I saw a hole in my chest the size of a silver dollar, no bleeding. The medic told me I wasn't bleeding because I had been hit by a large piece of shrapnel that was still red hot and had sealed my blood vessels as it entered my body.'

Pte Stanley Stypulowski, 16th Inf Regt, US 1st Inf Div (3)

'Shells were continually landing all about me and fragments from an 88mm which exploded about twenty yards in front of me hit me in the left cheek. It felt like being hit by a baseball bat, only the results were much worse. My upper jaw was shattered, my left cheek blown open. My upper lip was cut in half, the roof of my mouth was cut up and teeth and gums were lying on my tongue. I washed my face in cold Channel water and somehow managed not to pass out...

'I then found my best buddy, Pfc Robert Garbett, lying face down and dead. My adrenalin was pumping and I got up to cross the road above the wall ... A mortar shell exploded and three pieces of shrapnel got me in the left side of the head. My helmet had three holes, but probably saved me from much worse ... One of the medics, Cecil Breeden, leaned over me, shells and bullets flying, and applied a pressure bandage and sprinkled sulfa powder to my face wound. I tried to pull him down to safety, but he ... said, "You're hurt now. When I get it, you can take care of me."'

Pte Hal Baumgarten, 1st Bn, 116th Inf Regt, US 29th Inf Div (6)

'Franks and I walked out to the carnage in the road. The first person I saw was a German virtually burnt and blown to pieces. He was still alive and ... pointed to my automatic and to himself. It was obvious that he wanted me to kill him and take him out of his pain. To this day, I regret I did not.'

Capt Jack Hart, 78th Armd Field Arty Bn, US 2nd Armd Div (7)

'We began to get a number of medical cases officially termed "battle exhaustion". Some of these were undoubtedly men whose minds had been disturbed by intensive shellfire. But others were the weaker brethren who lacked the necessary strength of will to keep going, when exhausted by lack of sleep and tested by shelling and mortaring and all the other unpleasantness of war ... Later I made it a rule that exhaustion cases were only to be evacuated to B Echelon (transport lines) where our good Doctor Dickie Williams treated them with sleeping pills and in a few days they were back with their Companies. I emphasised the value of sleep before battle. We developed a drill to ensure this (battles are often fought by tired men). Battle exhaustion cases became rare.'

Maj George Taylor, 1st Bn, Worcestershire Regt, British 43rd Inf Div (8)

(US National Archives)

'He was half way across the field when he heard it coming. If he had fallen flat he might have got away with a couple of shrapnel wounds. But he didn't. He turned to run back to the trench. The shell hit him. I'm telling you, IT BLEW HIM TO TINY LITTLE BITS! I've seen things up there, sir, that I never want to describe or remember, but if you can picture a booted foot, a section of the human cranium, a bunch of fingers, a bit of clothing, you can get some idea — it was simply a matter of little tiny bits.'

Anonymous British private, Worcestershire Regt (9)

'A chap was brought in with the top of his head blown off, brains spilling out into the stretcher. The MO took one look at him. I said, "Is there anything we can do?" He shrugged. So I gave him a lethal shot of morphine. When the MO came back, I told him. He said, "It's OK, you did quite right. If he'd lived, he'd have been a vegetable for the rest of his days." I am sure there were others like this. But we did not talk about it.'

Pte James Bramwell, 9th Parachute Bn, British 6th Abn Div (10)

'Nothing had prepared me ... for what happened next. The leading section commander was attempting to scramble through the barbed wire ... a single enemy bullet pierced his belly and as a result exploded a phosphorus grenade he carried in his webbing pouch. Struggling in desperation he became entangled in the barbed wire and hung there, a living, screaming human beacon. His only release from the fiery hell, as he must have known, was to plead for someone to shoot him as quickly and mercifully as possible.

'A single well-aimed bullet from a compassionate but no doubt appalled officer put the lad out of his blazing hell. Even in death the horror continued as the phosphorus burned into the now mercifully lifeless body. Many a silent prayer was murmured as we witnessed our comrade's instant funeral pyre. His manner of death was a salutary lesson to us all — never again did we carry phosphorus grenades in our webbing pouches'.

Cpl Douglas Proctor, 4th Bn, Somerset Light Infantry, British 43rd Inf Div (11)

'Sure enough we found a poor little chap with both legs blown off above the knees, moaning softly and, I remember, he was saying "Oh dear! Oh dear!" The stretcher-bearer shook his head and, I thought, looked pointedly at my revolver.'

Maj Brodie, British 51st Highland Div (12)

A cigarette was the first thing most wounded men craved as soon as they had been bandaged. Most soldiers of the armies of World War II smoked heavily, and cigarettes were issued free as being important for morale. (IWM B5524)

'Because I was part of the Brigadier's Tactical HQ ... I could see the effect of casualties on the battalions. By the end of June, 50 Div had lost, killed, wounded and missing, over 300 officers and 3,000 soldiers. Reinforcements came up every night to plug the holes before the next day's attack. The ... courage was still there, but the skills were going, and it showed. If our own artillery or mortar fire failed to dislodge the enemy, our infantry seemed ... at a loss about what to do ... Untrained or semi-skilled 3-inch mortarmen would fire their mortars from underneath trees, killing themselves with their own bombs exploding in the branches above.

'I began to see worrying signs in my own company. Because there were four brigades in the Division, and only three machine-gun companies, we never got a rest. My soldiers had been with me right through the Desert, the invasion of Sicily and now Normandy. Battle fatigue was beginning to show in one or two cases. A superb corporal suddenly broke into tears and had to be sent back. His reserve of courage had run out; he had been at it too long.'

Maj Peter Martin, 151 Inf Bde, British 50th Inf Div (13)

(Tim Hawkins)

'France 29 June

Dear Dorothy,
Had a drop of "Homemade French Champ-
agne Brandy" last night — whoosh —
nearly lifted my head off.

'We have got a cow — poor dear
mooing its head off full of milk and shrap-
nel — and then it gets milked about every
half-hour — still, makes the old cup of tea
taste good.

'Do you remember Jack Atherton? He
and his wife had dinner with us in the
Fleur de Lys in Sandwich about two years
ago ... he was a bit unlucky the night
before last and was killed.

'I am very well Dot so there is no
need for you to worry at all — only thing
is I really would like a good bath ...'
Letter to his wife from Lt Col Gerald
Tilly, 4th Bn, Dorsetshire Regt, British
43rd Inf Div. See page 101 for the cir-
cumstances of Lt Col Atherton's death. (3)

(Courtesy Ed Storey)

'10 July 1944

Dear Mother,
I feel like a heel for not writing regularly
to you and I know how anxious I would
feel if I didn't hear from you. Please never
stop writing dear.

'I cannot tell you much about what is
going on over here, as we haven't been
very far inland and cannot tell about the
people or the country either. I can say this
though: it is a gigantic business and we
are fighting a tough enemy.

'Mother, before I close for a while, I
am a bit mixed up about things but am
straight on this: Dad and you are my
ideal couple. If I can be half the man Dad
is and have the outlook you have on life, I
won't ever have to worry. I have been
scared and I guess there will be plenty of
times in the future when I will be scared,
but as long as I don't let you, Dad, Dot,
Rich and David down, I shall be happy,
no matter the outcome of this do ... Will
say cheerio for now, sweetheart.
All best love,
Art'
Letter from anonymous soldier of
Canadian 3rd Inf Div (4)

(Simon Pugh-Jones)

Bibliography & Sources

Ambrose, Stephen E., *D-Day June 6 1944: The Climactic Battle of World War II*, Touchstone Books/Simon & Schuster, 1995

Bagnall, S., *The Attack*, Hamish Hamilton, 1947

Bando, Mark, *Breakout at Normandy*, MBI Publishing, Osceola, WI, 1999

Berlin, Stephen, *I Am Lazarus*, Galley Press, 1961

Blumenson, Martin, *Rommel's Last Victory*, Allen & Unwin, 1968

Borthwick, Alastair, *Battalion*, Bâton Wicks, 1994

Burgett, Donald, *Currahee!*, Houghton Mifflin, Boston, 1967

Capa, Robert, *Slightly Out of Focus*, Henry Holt, NY, 1947

Cawthon, Charles R., *Other Clay: A Rembrance of the World War II Infantry*, University of Colorado Press, 1990

D-Day Museum, Portsmouth, England

Delaforce, Patrick, *The Fighting Wessex Wyverns: From Normandy to Bremerhaven with the 43rd Wessex Division*, Alan Sutton, 1994

Eisenhower Center archive, University of New Orleans

Ellis, John, *The Sharp End*, Windrow & Greene, 1990

Ewing, Joseph, *29, Let's Go!*, Infantry Journal Press, Washington DC, 1948

Fane, Francis, *Naked Warriors*, Prentice Hall, NY, 1956

Flower, James & Reeves, Desmond, ed., *The War 1939-45*, Cassell

Gardiner, Juliet, *D-Day: Those Who Were There*, Collins & Brown, 1994

Giles, J., *The GI Journal of Sergeant Giles*, Houghton Mifflin, Boston, n.d.

Grant, Douglas, *The Fuel of the Fire*, Cresset, n.d.

Grant, R., *The 51st Highland Division at War*, Ian Allan, 1977

Henry, Mark, *The US Army in World War II (1)*, Osprey, 2000

Hoover Institution archive, Stanford, California

Imperial War Museum archive, London

Infantry magazine, USA

Irving, David, *The War Between the Generals*, Allen Lane

Jary, Sydney, *18 Platoon*, Sydney Jary Ltd, 9 Upper Belgrave Rd, Clifton, Bristol BS8 2XH, 1987

Koskimaki, George E., *D-Day with the Screaming Eagles*, Vantage Press, NY, 1970

Lewis, Jon E., ed., *The Mammoth Book of War Diaries & Letters*, Robinson, 1998

Liddell Hart Centre for Military Archives, King's College, London

Lindsay, M., *So Few Got Through*, Arrow Books, 1956

Lovat, The Lord, *March Past*, Weidenfeld & Nicholson, 1978

Lucas, James, *The British Soldier*, Arms & Armour Press, 1989

McKee, Alexander, *Caen: Anvil of Victory*, Pan Books, 1966

Miller, Russell, *Nothing Less than Victory*, Michael Joseph, 1993

Muir, A., *The First of Foot*, private publication, 1961

Neillands, Robin & De Normann, Roderick, *D-Day 1944: Voices from Normandy*, Orion Books, 1994

Proctor, Douglas, *Section Commander*, Dept of War Studies, Royal Military Academy Sandhurst, n.d.

Pyle, Ernie, *Brave Men*, Henry Holt, NY, 1944

Simpson, Louis, *Air With Armed Men*, London Magazine Editions, 1972

Slaughter, J. R., *Wartime Memories of John R. Slaughter*, Eisenhower Center, U. of New Orleans

Thompson, Julian, *The Imperial War Museum Book of Victory in Europe*, Sidgwick & Jackson, 1995

Tute, Warren, with Costello, John, & Hughes, Terry, *D-Day*, Sidgwick & Jackson, 1974

US Army Military History Institute archive, Carlisle, Pensylvania

US National Archives, Washington, DC

US War Department, *St Lô*, n.d.

Warner, Philip, *The D-Day Landings*, William Kimber, 1980

Weir, John S., *The Tyranny of Fear*, Vantage Press, NY, 1979

Wilson, George, *If You Survive*, Ivy Ballantine Books, NY, 1987

The World at War, Thames Television series, London

Whiting, Charles, *'44: In Combat on the Western Front from Normandy to the Ardennes*, Book Club Associates, 1984

Wynberg, S. K., 'The Combat Neurosis', *American Journal of Sociology, Vol.51*, 1946

Source Notes

GETTING READY
(1) Eisenhower Center
(2) 'As Mac Saw It', typescript,
    US Military History Institute archive
(3) 'As Mac Saw It', typescript,
US Military History Institute archive
(4) 'A Yank In Britain', typescript, Hoover
    Institution archive
(5) Eisenhower Center
(6) Cawthon, C.R.
(7) Delaforce, P.
(8) Eisenhower Center
(9) Cawthon, C.R.
(10) Miller, R., interview
(11) D-Day Museum
(12) Imperial War Museum archive
(13) Eisenhower Center
(14) Delaforce, P.
(15) Eisenhower Center, Slaughter memoir
(16) Eisenhower Center
(17) Eisenhower Center
(18) Eisenhower Center
(19) Delaforce, P.
(20) Miller, R., interview
(21) Thompson, J.
(22) Eisenhower Center, Slaughter memoir
(23) Warner, P.
(24) Warner, P.
(25) Warner, P.
(26) Warner, P.
(27) Thompson, J.
(28) Thompson, J.
(29) Thompson, J.
(30) Thompson, J.
(31) Gardiner, J.
(32) Eisenhower Center
(33) Giles, J.
(34) Eisenhower Center

GETTING THERE — By Air:
US Airborne
(1) Miller, R.
(2) Rapport, Leonard, et al, *Rendezvous
with Destiny*, quoted Miller, R., p.179
(3) Robert W.McCormick archive,
    US Military History Institute
(4) Burgett, D.
(5) *The World at War*, Thames Television
(6) Neillands & De Normann
(7) Koskimaki, G.
(8) Neillands & De Normannn
(9) Neillands & De Normann
(10) Neillands & De Norman
(11) Neillands & De Normann
(12) Robert W.McCormick archive,
     US Military History Institute
(13) Eisenhower Center
(14) Gardiner, J.
(15) Eisenhower Center
(16) Miller, R., interview
(17) Eisenhower Center
(18) Eisenhower Center
(19) Miller, R.

(20) Eisenhower Center
(21) Neillands & De Normann
(22) Neilands & De Normann
(23) Miller, R.
(24) Neillands & De Normann
(25) Eisenhower Center
(26) Eisenhower Center

British & Canadian Airborne
(1) Miller, R.
(2) Thompson, J.
(3) Warner, P.
(4) Thompson, J.
(5) Warner, P.
(6) Ncillands & De Normann
(7) Warner, P.
(8) Warner, P.
(9) Thompson, J.
(10) Warner, P.
(11) Neillands & De Normann
(12) Warner, P.
(13) Neillands & De Normann
(14) Warner, P.
(15) Neillands & De Normann
(16) Neillands & De Normann
(17) Thompson, J.

GETTING THERE — By Sea:
The Crossing
(1) Capa, R.
(2) *The World at War*, Thames Television
(3) Miller, R., interview
(4) Lovat, The Lord
(5) Pyle, E.
(6) MS, Liddell Hart Centre for Military
    Archives
(7) Ewing, J.
(8) Eisenhower Center
(9) Miller, R.
(10) Eisenhower Center, Slaughter memoir
(11) Cawthon, C.R.
(12) Eisenhower Center, Slaughter memoir

The American Beaches
(1) Neillands & De Normann
(2) Eisenhower Center
(3) Eisenhower Center
(4) Neillands & De Normann
(5) Eisenhower Center
(6) D-Day Museum, Portsmouth
(7) Eisenhower Center
(8) Fane, F.
(9) Gardiner, J.
(10) Eisenhower Center
(11) Cawthon, C.R.
(12) Gardiner, J.
(13) Eisenhower Center
(14) *The World at War*, Thames Television
(15) Cawthon, C.R.
(16) Eisenhower Center, Slaughter memoir
(17) Neillands & De Normann
(18) *The World at War*, Thames Television
(19) Gardiner, J.

(20) Eisenhower Center, Slaughter memoir
(21) Eisenhower Center, Slaughter memoir
(22) Eisenhower Center
(23) Eisenhower Center
(24) Gardiner, J.
(25) US National Archives
(26) Eisenhower Center
(27) Eisenhower Center
(28) *Infantry*, May-June 1985
(29) Eisenhower Center
(30) Cawthon, C.R.

The British & Canadian Beaches
(1) Warner, P.
(2) Warner, P.
(3) Warner, P.
(4) Warner, P.
(5) Thompson, J.
(6) Warner, P.
(7) Warner, P.
(8) Warner, P.
(9) Warner, P.
(10) Warner, P.
(11) Miller, R., interview
(12) Neillands & De Normann
(13) Neillands & De Normann
(14) Neillands & De Normann
(15) Neillands & De Normann
(16) Neillands & De Normann
(17) Neillands & De Normann
(18) Warner, P.
(19) Thompson, J.
(20) Thompson, J.
(21) Warner, P.
(22) Warner, P.
(23) Warner, P.
(24) Warner, P.
(25) Grant, D.
(26) Warner, P.
(27) Warner, P.
(28) Warner, P.
(29) Neillands & De Normann

STAYING THERE
(1) Borthwick, A.
(2) Proctor, D.

The Enemy
(1) Bando, M.
(2) Warner, P.
(3) Delaforce, P.
(4) Borthwick, A.
(5) Warner, P.
(6) Delaforce, P.
(7) Thompson, J.
(8) Bando, M.
(9) Bando, M.
(10) Delaforce, P.
(11) Thompson, J.
(12) Jary, S.

The American Front
(1) Neillands & De Normann
(2) Gardiner, J.
(3) Eisenhower Center
(4) Flower & Reeves, ed
(5) Weir, J.S.
(6) Bando, M.
(7) Bando, M.
(8) Simpson, L.
(9) *St Lô*, US War Dept
(10) Bando, M.
(11) Bando, M.
(12) Weir, J.S.
(13) Bando, M.
(14) Bando, M.
(15) Wilson, G.
(16) Bando, M.
(17) Bando, M.
(18) Anon., quoted Flower & Reeves, ed

Tanks in the Bocage
(1) Bando, M.
(2) Wilson, G.
(3) Thompson, J.
(4) Irving, D.
(5) Delaforce, P.
(6) Thompson, J.
(7) Thompson, J.
(8) Bando, M.
(9) Warner, P.
(10) Thompson, J.
(11) Thompson, J.
(12) Thompson, J.
(13) Thompson, J.
(14) McKee, A.
(15) Delaforce, P.
(16) Delaforce, P.
(17) Thompson, J.
(18) Blumenson, M.
(19) Bando, M.
(20) Thompson, J.
(21) Delaforce, P.
(22) Lucas, J.
(23) Delaforce, P.

The British Front
(1) Delaforce, P.
(2) Delaforce, P.
(3) Proctor, D.
(4) Muir, A.
(5) Thompson, J.
(6) Delaforce, P.
(7) Bagnall, S.
(8) Delaforce, P.
(9) Delaforce, P.
(10) Delaforce, P.
(11) Delaforce, P.
(12) Delaforce, P.
(13) Delaforce, P.
(14) Borthwick, A.
(15) Delaforce, P.
(16) Borthwick, A.

(17) Borthwick, A.
(18) Delaforce, P.
(19) Delaforce, P.
(20) Delaforce, P.
(21) Delaforce, P.
(22) Delaforce, P.
(23) Delaforce, P.
(24) Thompson, J.
(25) Delaforce, P.
(26) Proctor, D.
(27) Delaforce, P.
(28) Delaforce, P.
(29) Delaforce, P.
(30) Delaforce, P.
(31) Delaforce, P.
(32) Jary, S.
(33) Proctor, D.
(34) Delaforce, P.
(35) Delaforce, P.
(36) Delaforce, P.
(37) Delaforce, P.
(38) Delaforce, P.
(39) Irving, D.

Casualties
(1) Ellis, J.
(2) Delaforce, P.
(3) Eisenhower Center
(4) Lindsay, M.
(5) Warner, P.
(6) Eisenhower Center,
    Slaughter memoir
(7) Bando, M.
(8) Delaforce, P.
(9) Berlin, S.
(10) Thompson, J.
(11) Proctor, D.
(12) Grant, R.
(13) Thompson, J.
(14) Wynberg, S.K.

Air Support
(1) Pyle, E.
(2) Borthwick A.

Front Line Rations
(1) Borthwick, A.
(2) Henry, M.

Civilians
(1) Irving, D.
(2) Delaforce, P.

Letters Home
(1) Bando, M.
(2) Lewis, J.E. ed
(3) Imperial War Museum archive
(4) Imperial War Museum archive

Glossary

AP	Armour piercing ammunition - solid shot relying on kinetic energy to pierce armour plate
Bangalore torpedo	Long tube-shaped explosive charge for cutting through barbed wire entanglements
Battalion	Military unit, usually of about 800 men commanded by a lieutenant-colonel
Bren gun	British light machine gun, issued one per ten-man infantry section
Brigade	Military formation, usually of three battalions
Commando	British battalion, of men selected for fitness and aggression and trained in advanced infantry skills
Company	Military sub-unit of between 100 and 200 men commanded by a major or captain; three or four made up a battalion
CV	Command vehicle - lightly armoured truck acting as the mobile command centre for a unit
Division	Military formation, usually of three brigades or regiments, totalling between 10,000 and 14,000 men - airborne divisions were smaller. Allied infantry divisions had nine infantry battalions plus integral artillery, engineer, armoured reconnaissance and other supporting units. Armoured divisions usually had three tank battalions (in British parlance, 'regiments') each with 50 to 70 tanks, three motorised or mechanised infantry battalions, and motorised or mechanised supporting units
Doover	British slang for a slit-trench improved by the occupants for use over more than a brief period
ENSA	British organisation providing entertainers to put on shows for the troops when out of the line
Harbour	Overnight camp of a tank unit (also 'laager')
Hay box	Box packed with hay to insulate food containers
HE	High explosive artillery ammunition
Heath Robinson	British cartoonist of fantastically over-complex machinery: thus, any improvised device whose appearance did not command confidence
KIA	Killed in action
Moaning Minnie	British slang for German Nebelwerfer multiple barrel rocket-propelled mortar
MM	Military Medal - respected British gallantry decoration for non-officer ranks
O-group	Orders group - gathering of officers for passing of orders for next tasks
Platoon	Military sub-unit of 30 to 40 men led by a lieutenant or senior NCO; three or four platoons usually made up a company
RAP	Regimental Aid Post - the basic aid station run by a unit medical officer, for immediate treatment before casualty evacuation
Rangers	US Army equivalent of British Commandos
Regiment	US Army unit of three battalions; British armoured or artillery unit equivalent to a battalion strength
Screaming Meemie	US slang - see 'Moaning Minnie'
Spandau	Allied soldiers' generic term for German machine guns
Stick	A single plane-load of paratroopers

'Before I got hit with fragments, I was confident all right. I thought the others might get hurt but not me. Then a sniper's bullet got me and that shook my confidence right there. I knew my number could be up, too. I got better, came back, and was going on for a while; but I was not as cocky as I used to be. Then some buddies of mine got it, and that wore me down more. "My number's coming," I felt it in my stomach ... Then during a shelling, a blast came near me and I was hit by fragments. It shook me so badly; I thought it was my time now. But I jumped up and tried to shoot ... I don't know what happened after. I must have blacked out or something. I came to in the hospital ...'

Anonymous US infantryman (14)

(Simon Pugh-Jones)

123

Letters Home

Soldiers' letters home were censored to remove any information which might be of possible value to the enemy, including all mention of places, dates, units or identifiable events. The contents are therefore usually banal — but none the less poignant for that, when one considers the lives these men were often leading when they found themselves a moment of privacy to write them. Apart from the universal human yearning for any kind of contact with their loved ones, they are touching in their obvious determination not to add to their families' anxiety by any description of the actual horrors and hardships of war. These few representative examples, from American GIs, a British officer and a Canadian infantryman, are perhaps typical enough of common preoccupations, however differently expressed.

(IWM B11766)

'25 July 1944
My Dearest Mary,
How is my little girl today? For myself, fine and enjoying a beautiful day. We woke up this morning having an apple fight with another crew. There are plenty of little green apples here and I would bet that we have thrown a GI truckload of them. Some of the boys play cards, read and sleep. We are eating B rations now and the food is OK. By the way, steak is a very common dish at the front. When a cow gets hit, it hardly has time to die before it is in the frying pan being cooked. Well, the medical officer has to put his OK on it first ...

'I must close as there is no news here. I love and miss you more each day ... So answer soon with a long letter. Remember, there will be times that I can't write but don't think that I won't be thinking of you for you are always on my mind. I will say Bye now.
With all my love,
Douglas'
Letter to his girlfriend from Douglas Tanner, 1/67th Armd Regt, US 2nd Armd Div, on the eve of Operation 'Cobra' (1)

'18 June

Dear Mom,
We get milk and cider off these French people. It looks like they are very glad to see us yanks. They should be these dirty Germans tried to make slaves out of them. I met a little boy I used to go to school with on the boat crossing the channel. There is lots of things I would like to tell you but maybe later I will be able to. I still have my little prayer book and I have used it. I am sure it has done me lots of good, you know what I mean ...
Take care of yourself,
love,
Son'
Letter from an anonymous GI to his mother (2)